Slave Law in the Americas

Slave Law
in the Americas,

ALAN WATSON

THE UNIVERSITY OF GEORGIA PRESS
Athens and London

© 1989 by the University of Georgia Press
Athens, Georgia 30602
All rights reserved

Designed by Nighthawk Design
Set in 10 on 13 Linotron 202 Sabon
Typeset by The Composing Room of Michigan, Inc.
Printed and bound by Thomson-Shore

The paper in this book meets the guidelines for
permanence and durability of the Committee on
Production Guidelines for Book Longevity of the
Council on Library Resources.

Printed in the United States of America

93   92   91   90   89   5   4   3   2   1

Library of Congress Cataloging in Publication Data

Watson, Alan.
    Slave law in the Americas / Alan Watson.
      p.   cm.
    Bibliography: p.
    Includes index.
    ISBN 0-8203-1179-0 (alk. paper)
      1. Slavery—Law and legislation—America—History.   2. Roman
law—Reception—Europe—History.   I. Title.
KDZ546.W38   1989
342.7'087—dc20
[347.0287]   89-4958
                                                                        CIP

British Library Cataloging in Publication Data available

For Alan, Irvine,
Roddy, John, and Allan

CONTENTS

PREFACE

I began writing this book in 1967 but had trouble completing it because of the lack of a general theory of why law changes and how law relates to society. Comparative legal history is in its infancy. But without a theory of change based on historical evidence the significance of similarities and differences in law cannot be evaluated. In Chapter 1 I present my general thesis. The book is as much about the nature of comparative law and its role in understanding law in society as it is about the specific subject of the law of slavery.

My interpretation of slave law in the various societies examined differs from that of other scholars. In general I have preferred not to point out the contrast but to concentrate instead on setting out and explaining the main primary sources of slave law. Since many of these sources are not readily available, I have given extensive quotations. The translations are my own.

Over the years I have incurred too many debts to too many friends to record. But John W. Cairns, Paul Finkelman, Bradley Nicholson, and Joseph W. McKnight read the entire typescript and gave me very helpful criticism. The Biddle Law Library of the University of Pennsylvania Law School was relentless in providing me with books, especially the secondary literature. In this regard the foreign law librarians, Marta Tarnowski and Maria Smolka-Day, deserve special thanks. The National Library of Scotland, the Max-Planck-Institut für europäische Rechtsgeschichte in Frankfurt-am-Main, and the Library of Congress provided me with all the older works that I could not otherwise find. To these institutions, their directors, and staff, I am enormously grateful. Likewise, I am deeply in the debt of my secretary, Deborah Nearey-Walsh, who coped cheerfully as draft followed draft.

I have avoided the use of abbreviations for legal sources and books except for a very few standard references to Roman law sources that I have frequently cited. These are as follows:

C.	The *Code* of Justinian
C. *Th.*	The *Code* of Theodosian
D.	The *Digest* of Justinian
G.	The *Institutes* of Gaius
J.	The *Institutes* of Justinian
pr.	*principium* (the first, unnumbered part of a text in some Roman sources)

INTRODUCTION

The main focus of this study in comparative law is the understanding of slave law in the Americas. Why was it so different in English America and in Latin America?

Comparative law is valuable in academic study because it helps to identify the circumstances in which law changes and hence to uncover the reasons for legal development. It illuminates the interest and role of governments in lawmaking. Consequently, comparative law tells us much about the relationship of law, legal rules, and institutions to the societies in which they operate. An understanding of this relationship is needed before one can draw any conclusions about a society from its legal rules and institutions. On this basis of comparative law, I set out in the first chapter a general theory of the development of private law, which I think is valid at least for all Western legal systems. The theory, in addition to what it may tell about law and society, also has considerable explanatory value for legal history.

To understand slave law in the Americas, one must know its forerunners in Europe, especially Roman law. In this book I set out briefly the law of slavery in ancient Rome and parts of America, where slaves have constituted a major proportion of the work force. I seek to explain, in the light of the general theory of the first chapter, why the rules were as they were. Each society is studied only for the time span in which slavery flourished as a social institution.[1]

The law surrounding slavery raises issues of the greatest moral, economic, political, and social significance. Hence the aspects of slave law I have chosen to emphasize are those that ought to throw most light on the nature of the individual society: the ease or difficulty of manumission and the acceptance of the former slave into the free society; restrictions on the owner's punishing or ill-treating his slave; the treatment of slaves by the criminal law; and the extent to which slaves are accorded legal personality.

This book has limited aims. Though I hope to cast some light on historical aspects of society in the Americas, I am in no sense a social historian, far less a comparative social historian. I do hope, though, that the information in the book will be useful to comparative social historians who wish to take account of the law.

The study of legal rules has traditionally occupied a prominent place in accounts of American slaveowning societies,[2] in part because it is easier to discover what the law was and to estimate how racist it appears to have been than it is to find out about other conditions of society. So I wish to indicate in the book that legal institutions and legal rules must be used with extreme caution in determining even fundamental societal values. My point is not that "law in action" is not necessarily the same as "law in books," but that "law in books," which, of course, at the very least, has a powerful impact on "law in action," may reflect something very different from the ethos of the society at large or of its ruling elite. In some circumstances knowledge of a society's law may give a very misleading picture of the society. Conclusions can be drawn about a society from its legal rules only after one has studied the setting, including the cultural setting, in which the rules were devised.

Another aim of this book is to call attention to the impact law has on society. This seems so obvious that it should not need to be mentioned were it not that, as I claim, much of law is determined by conditions outside of the society. No one, I think, will deny that the ease or difficulty of manumitting slaves had profound effects on the society at large. It is truly awesome if, as I shall argue, the relative ease with which masters could free slaves in Spanish, French, Portuguese, and Dutch America compared with English America was the result of differences in the legal tradition in Europe rather than societal conditions in the Americas. Yet the evidence shows that it is presumptuous to believe otherwise. If England had undergone a Reception of Roman law, then in English America there would have been fewer restrictions on masters freeing their slaves; there would have been more slaves freed; there would have been more blacks with access to money and property; and freed blacks would have been accepted as citizens. What a pointless and absurd tragedy the

United States has undergone, and is still undergoing, if this thesis is, as I insist, correct.

The hopes I have had for this book have changed over time. When I first began to work on comparative slave law in New Orleans in 1967, I was much under the influence of Frank Tannenbaum's path-breaking book, *Slave and Citizen: The Negro in the Americas.*[3] Using many of the same materials, I have reached different conclusions.[4] I was much intrigued by Stanley Elkins's *Slavery, a Problem in American Institutional and Intellectual Life,*[5] especially by the contrast he draws between the ease of manumitting slaves and their acceptance into free society in Latin America and the difficulty of manumission and greater discrimination against free blacks in English America.[6] These differences, or supposed differences, have long attracted scholars. Strong and subtle theories have been produced in explanation, often containing the same elements in varying proportions. One apparently plausible element is the role and power of the Roman Catholic church in Latin America in insisting that slaves were human beings with souls. In caring for souls, the argument goes, the church took away some of the domination of the master. For instance, to avoid the sin of fornication, slave marriage had to be recognized (giving slaves some element of personality). For the same reason slave marriages had to be preserved, thus slave husband and wife could not be sold separately.[7] Another apparently plausible element concerns the proportion of white women to white men. The lower the proportion—and in general throughout Latin America it was lower than in English America—the more open and (ultimately) the more respectable would be sexual relationships, not necessarily excluding marriage, between black and white. And the more respectable such relationships became, the more socially acceptable the offspring of mixed race would be. There are many other historical explanations of the differences in the ease of manumission and the acceptance of freed persons in free society, including indeed some based on the impact of law.[8] In this work I have sought to give an explanation only of the differences in the actual law. The explanation is based on the nature of legal culture and legal tradition. The thesis propounded is in no sense intended to be a complete explanation of the resultant differences in law, but, I submit, it is a sufficient explanation. I have deliberately excluded social history as far as possible though I am well aware that social conditions varied greatly from one place to another. I have no intention of denying that social, political, economic, and religious factors have an impact on legal development. But I want to bring into sharp focus the overriding thesis of the book: that the legal culture and legal tradition themselves can provide a sufficient explanation for the main features of a legal institution.

Though I have something to say about the slaves who were freed and to that extent discuss "law in action," I have nothing to say in general about the relative levels of manumission, the relative cruelties of owners, the relative levels of social acceptability of freed slaves into the free society, and the relative level of racism in the various states. Although I have come to be very skeptical about the distinctions drawn by many scholars on the differences in social attitude to blacks in Latin and English America, I have found no way to progress from comparative law to comparative social attitudes and even to comparative social history. Indeed, I see no way to progress from comparative social fact to comparative social attitudes.

An example might explain this difficulty in using evidence. At most places at most times a reasonably economic owner would be conscious of the chattel value of slaves and thus would ensure some care in their treatment. In Roman Egypt, few slaves worked as agricultural laborers, the most dangerous and lowly job of all. That was reserved for free persons.[9] In his work on Roman agriculture, Varro in the first century B.C. advised that it was more profitable to work unhealthy lands with hired laborers than with slaves and that even on healthy land it was more profitable to use hired labor for the heaviest work.[10] In English America, some owners inserted clauses in contracts hiring out slaves forbidding the hirer to use the slaves for specific dangerous tasks such as getting into the water to help release a riverboat stuck in the mud.[11] But someone had to undertake these tasks. But on occasion circumstances might be different. Assume that part of state X is given over to sugar production, that there is a semipermanent shortage of slaves, and that free persons cannot be found to do the work. Work in the sugar fields is unremitting. At harvest time, boiling the sugar is a nonstop process that continues all night. The production line cannot easily be stopped or slowed. Appalling economic logic—if the price for sugar is right— then may take over.[12] Slaves will be forced to work harder and for much longer hours. Accidents will be more common. The death rate will be much higher. The birth rate will be much lower: there may be relatively fewer female slaves[13] because there is less of an economic need for them, there will be less opportunity for family life, there will be more miscarriages because of the harshness of the work and more abortions because of the perceived difficulties in child rearing. There will be greater infant mortality both because of the weaker health of mother and child at birth and because there will be less time available to care for children. To preserve some degree of sanity, owners will distance themselves even further psychologically from slaves and regard them even less as people. Consequently, and because there is a real need for the slave labor force, there will be no or almost no manumissions. In the absence of important positive rewards for hard work, discipline will be harsher. If statistics on slavery were kept in that part of state X and one had information on the level of protest in the state, on legal changes that were proposed perhaps successfully, and so forth, then one might be able to say something about social attitudes to slavery (or slavery in that form) in state X. But if one also had statistics on slavery from state Y, which did not produce sugar, and these differed in any significant way from those from state X, then I do not know how these facts could be used to say anything meaningful about comparative social attitudes in the two societies. Too many of the variables would differ.

Discussion of slave law "in books" will not by itself reveal the dynamics of slavery. And slave law, not the dynamics of slavery, is the subject of this book. But the law, including the slave law, in any society is artificial in the sense that the rules in existence, the way they are created and the reasoning applied to their discovery do not always or necessarily correspond to the economic, political, or social contours of the society. The extent to which even the law of slavery has a life of its own is one of the themes of this book.

Slave Law in the Americas

1

THE GENERAL THESIS

Law is power. Law is politics. Law is politics in the sense that it is the persons who have political power who determine which persons or bodies create law, how the validity of law is to be assessed, and how the legal order is to operate. But one cannot simply deduce, as is frequently assumed, that the holders of political power determine the rules and the sources of law. The lesson of history is that over most of the field of law and especially of private law, in most political and economic circumstances, rulers need have no interest in determining what the rules of law are or should be, provided always, of course, that revenues roll in and the public peace is kept. Rulers and their immediate underlings can be, and often have been and are, indifferent to the nature of the legal rules in operation. This simple fact is often overlooked; indeed, it is habitually denied. But failure to accept it is the greatest cause of misunderstanding the nature of law, the relationship of law and society, and the course of legal development.[1]

For Europe, the general accuracy of the proposition that the government[2] is usually uninterested in the precise nature of most of the legal rules in operation is easily demonstrated by facts that, I think, no serious legal scholar would consider denying, but which are not usually considered together. First, ancient Rome's system of private law is regarded as the most innovative (and influential) the world has ever known. But during its most formative time, the last two centuries of the republic and the first two and a half centuries of the empire, it was mainly the work of the jurists, private individuals who, in that capacity, had no ties to government.[3] Second, from the eleventh century until the modern era of codification, the main feature of legal development in continental Europe was the Reception of Roman law.[4] This could only occur, as it did, in the absence of legislation introducing much new law on a different basis. It resulted above all from the work and the interpretation of professors who again, as such, had no (necessary) ties to government. The Reception was seldom imposed by rulers; when it was, it was usually a recognition of the status quo. Moreover, what was imposed was the *Corpus Juris Civilis* as a whole or as glossed, not just the rules favorable to princes. But in general the Reception occurred at a lower level because the courts accepted Roman rules.[5]

Third, there was a paucity of legislation on private law during the same period. This cannot be, as some will have it, because of a lack of power or authority to legislate, because the same times and places saw much legislation on other matters. Fourth, feudalism, as a social and military system, was coming to an end in the twelfth century or soon thereafter, but it was only then that the feudal law (as set out in the *Libri Feudorum*), which was to be very influential, was coming into being.[6] Yet though it involves a great degree of decentralization, feudalism, of all social systems, should be the one that most reaches from the highest level of authority downward because of its nature of intense personal fealty.

Fifth, European rulers have often been indifferent to communicating clearly the substance of law, even of criminal law, to their subjects. This is seen, for instance, in the common scarcity of legislation and the consequent difficulty of finding or deducing the law from a mass of precedents or juristic writings. This lack is incomprehensible if rulers had much interest in the actual substance of the law.[7] Sixth, even great codifiers of private law such as Justinian and Frederick the Great were much more motivated by a desire to make law more accessible than to make it conform to a particular political or social ideal. Napoleon wanted there to be one law for all of France, and Atatürk wanted to modernize Turkey. The precise content of the law was generally of less concern.[8] Last (for the moment), in England from the origins of the common law until the second half of the nineteenth century, law was left to be developed mainly by judicial precedent.[9] Legal growth thus was haphazard, slow, unresponsive to social and political conditions, incomprehensible to non-lawyers, and unsystematic.

The lesson is twofold. Governments often do not legislate even on important matters. When they do, they frequently show little concern for the content of the rules they promulgate; indeed, they often borrow on a large scale from different societies.

But a politically and economically developed state needs legal rules. If the government will not make them, some other group has to and will: the jurists in ancient Rome; law professors in medieval and later continental Europe; judges in common law England. If the government is uninterested in the content of the legal rules, it is likely to be equally uninterested in determining who makes the rules or in setting out the conditions or circumstances in which they are made (provided, of course, that the government approves of the lawmakers). And the government can intervene when it wants to. The mode of lawmaking in vogue will be largely accidental. Thus, at Rome (except for the obscure, short-lived, and apparently unimportant *ius respondendi*), no one appointed jurists to be jurists. They were recognized to be such, because of their talents and social position, by others who had arrogated to themselves the status of jurist. That the opinion of a jurist was treated as having authority was itself accidental or, at least, was not the result of any choice or decision by the government and was the outcome of past history. In the fifth century B.C., the College of Pontiffs was given the sole right to interpret the law, and it delegated this duty to one of its members. Giving legal opinions conferred high status on the giver, and his opinion was authoritative. Men prominent in public life would wish to have the reputation of knowing the law. As the college's legal monopoly broke down, the social cachet of giving legal opinions continued, and opinions were still treated as having authority. The heroes of Roman law are jurists.[10]

In medieval and later Europe, though professors were appointed to university chairs, sometimes even by rulers, they were not appointed to make law. Their authority was purely a by-product of weight being given to the *Corpus Iuris Civilis.* The *Corpus Iuris,* a collection of old law, had to be interpreted, and the obvious people to understand it were not judges or practitioners but specifically appointed interpreters—professors. The Reception of Roman law and the lawmaking powers of the law professors go hand in hand. The heroes of Continental law before codification are law professors.

In England, though judges were officially appointed, no ruler actually gave judges the power to make law. Otherwise the notion could not have been so long maintained that judges were finders, not makers, of law. But in the absence of better guidance on how to reach their decision—and it is in the nature of law and legal reasoning to look for guidance inside the law or, if outside, in a system regarded as appropriate—judges will rely on previous judgments. And the process hardened. The heroes of the common law are judges.

Thus in Europe, lawmaking by persons other than the government was and is both common and the result of neglect. It is striking that the power to make law in these ways is the result of past history and for most of the time purely legal history. A particular Roman feature is worthy of note. In the later republic the other main factor in the development of private law was the edict of the praetor. Praetors were the second highest elected officials, ranking immediately below the consuls, and among other duties they, especially the urban and peregrine praetors, had control of the courts. All of the higher magistrates had the authority to issue edicts setting out their interpretation of their duties and how they would proceed in the exercise of their office. The praetors, too, issued edicts (which eventually became standard) setting out the actions they would allow in their courts. Technically, the praetors could not make law, but by granting, refusing, extending, and limiting remedies they were responsible for much legal change. The Edicts must be regarded as governmental lawmaking, though not by the government as a whole or the highest executive officers, but the system was never devised or planned to be such. It was an accidental by-product of the general executive powers given to all higher public officials; it was the result of neglect. In addition, the extreme brevity of the edictal statements of law and of the model forms of action, which are very uninformative as to the scope of the legal rules, are explicable only if one assumes there was cooperation between praetors and jurists. The jurists gave legal meaning to bare prescriptions which in all likelihood they also often suggested.[11] The praetor may be credited with introducing the contract of sale, of hire, and of partnership, but the substance of such contracts was entirely the work of the jurists.

But if much lawmaking is the result of neglect, then the lawmakers must be self-sustaining. For example, a jurist becomes a good jurist if his fellow jurists hold him in high regard. A jurist who was also an imperial bureaucrat might be able to persuade the emperor to issue a rescript settling a disputed point. But that would not make him a good jurist. It must be for this reason that many legal issues, described by the jurist Gaius in the mid–second century A.D. as the object of dispute between the rival schools, were unresolved centuries later in the time of Justinian: no jurist had the issue settled by asking for and obtaining an imperial ruling. A jurist might wish his opinion to prevail in court, but what he most wanted was the high regard of his fellow jurists, which he could not receive if the emperor intervened. Only on this basis can one see a need for Justinian's famous *Fifty Decisions,* which were a preliminary to his *Digest,* the great compilation of juristic writings. Their purpose was to settle disputes of the ancient classical jurists. It would appear that not one influential jurist (who was also a bureaucrat) had persuaded an emperor to give an authoritative ruling.[12] On different lines, a reading of the surviving juristic materials, including those in Justinian's *Digest,* leaves the impression that the jurists were profoundly indifferent to what actually happened in court.

But by the very fact of being self-sustaining, the legal elite come to treat law as their professional culture. Their reputation depends on the respect of their fellows, not on the respect of nonlawyers or even of lawyers who are not close to their group. They become uninterested in the views of others. No club is so intellectually exclusive as English higher court judges.[13] They increase their awareness of being an elite by distancing themselves from others, except those who might soon join them on the bench. To read Cicero is to gain the impression that, top orator and politician though he was, he felt excluded from the ranks of jurists. Though he received education in law from both Quintus Mucius Scaevola, the augur, who was consul in 117 B.C., and Quintus Mucius Scaevola, consul in 95, he was not regarded (and did not regard himself) as a jurist.[14] The remark of his jurist colleague in the praetorship, Aquillius Gallus, which he quotes, was not kindly meant: "Nihil hoc ad ius, ad Ciceronem" ("This has nothing to do with law, but with Cicero").[15] Cicero's own sneering at the science of law seems to be that of one who felt excluded.

The legal elite thus turns inward to seek a reputation. Discussion, argument, or invention, to be approved, must all take place within the rules of the game which the players fix for themselves. What these rules will be, even for one type of lawmakers such as judges, will vary from place to place and time to time, but rules of the game there will always be. These rules are not the result of decree—these lawmakers have no power to make general decrees—but emerge unconsciously or almost so, over a period, usually over a long period of time. Opinions of individual jurists or professors have to win general acceptance before they become legal rules. This acceptance has to be wrung from their fellows, and it can be wrung from them only on the basis of shared culture. Typically, legal development occurring in this way is slow. The contract of sale, for example, came into being at Rome before 200 B.C. Yet at least three hundred years later it was accepted on the basis of juristic opinion that the contract contained implied warranties against eviction and hidden defects. But the possibility of inherent warranties was known from the outset—they existed in *mancipatio,* the formal conveyance—and express warranties were habitually taken so we know warranties were wanted. Again, in a system based on precedent, many cases usually have to occur before a general rule can be observed to have emerged and very many more before an institution can be said to exist. The legal institution of contract can scarcely be said to have emerged in England before the nineteenth century, and then under the influence of German law. Yet contracts, as a separate branch of the law, had existed in ancient Rome and in much of continental Europe from medieval times and had flourished as law even in poor, remote

Scotland from the seventeenth century. Law made by jurists, professors, and judges is the result of the accretion of centuries. Just as
what is functional does not emerge at once, so what is dysfunctional
does not disappear even when there is no opposition. How, indeed,
can it? Since these lawmakers have not been given authority to make
law, they have not been given authority to unmake it. Roman *patria
potestas,* the lifelong power of the father, long outlived any desire—
so far as we can tell—for it, and it clearly was economically dysfunctional. For England, one may cite Benefit of Clergy, which, it
has been authoritatively claimed, for centuries turned criminal justice into a farce.[16]

It is in accord with this that such lawmakers often make little
distinction between past and present generations with regard to
their estimate of quality and respect. A Roman jurist of the second
century A.D. would cite Servius or Alfenus of the first century B.C. or
Labeo of the following century as confidently as he would cite his
contemporaries. The great Doctors of the Gloss and Bartolus were
still considered authoritative in the eighteenth century. And many
subsequent English generations knew the power of the judgment in
(to choose almost at random) *The Carrier's Case* (1473) 64 SS 30;
Purefoy v. *Rogers* (1671) 2 Wms Saund, 380; *Coggs* v. *Bernard*
(1703) 2 Ld Raym 909; and *Bradford Corporation* v. *Pickles*
[1895] AC 587. Subsequent generations do not always read the
opinion of a Roman jurist or of an Accursius or Bartolus or of a
common law precedent in the same way. But they regard themselves
as being in the same tradition as the previous great lawyer, treading
in his footsteps, directly influenced by his opinion, which they treat
as full of authority even if not definitive.

A first example of law as the culture of the lawmakers can be
chosen from the Roman juristic response to the decree of the senate
known as *senatus consultum Silanianum* of 10 A.D. The *senatus
consultum* provided that if an owner (*dominus*) was murdered, all
the slaves who lived under his roof were to be questioned under
torture and then executed; the opening of the will and acceptance of
the inheritance were forbidden before the torturing and execution of
the slaves (lest the slaves had become free as a result of being man-

umitted by the will); and a slave who revealed the killer of his master acquired his freedom by decree of the praetor.[17] The jurist Ulpian explains the rationale: "Since otherwise no home can be safe unless slaves at the risk of their own lives are compelled to guard their masters both from members of their household and from outsiders."[18] The measure is harsh, but it is a brilliant legal solution to a fear that must bedevil all slaveowning societies. For individuals in the slaveowning class there could be drawbacks, however, if they were heirs (and hence would be deprived of their slaves) or if their right in the slave was less than full ownership.

In the present context the issue is the juristic response. It is horrifying that the jurists treat the *senatus consultum* with everyday interpretation, like any innocuous law, sometimes to further the purpose of the *senatus consultum,* sometimes according to standards fixed in other contexts and with no apparent concern for the purpose of the *senatus consultum.* It is this juristically blinkered second approach that is interesting as an example of law as culture. Thus if there is a usufruct in slaves and the owner is killed, the slaves are tortured and executed;[19] if it is the usufructuary who is killed, the slaves are not tortured or executed.[20] This second decision would seem to defeat the purpose of the *senatus consultum* because the issue is the usufructuary who is murdered in his own home and the slaves are resident with him. He deserves protection as much as the owner, but his right is not ownership so he gets no protection. Nor should one feel that the usufructuary's economic interest in the slaves would be less than that of the bare owner: much would depend on the respective ages of usufructuary and owner and on the ages of the slaves.

Similarly, a slave under the control of a *bona fide possessor* will not be executed. But a possessor in good faith is someone who received the slave thinking in good faith that he was receiving ownership. Again, if a son under paternal power is killed, he is to be considered (for this purpose) as the *dominus.*[21] If he has been freed from paternal power, Marcellus is doubtful but Ulpian thinks he ought to be treated as *dominus,*[22] but not if he had been given in adoption.[23] Likewise, the *senatus consultum* does not apply if the murdered person was a foster child.[24] But in all these instances the killing would have occurred in the home of the *paterfamilias*, the head of the family (so there was no breach of affection between, say, father and the son given in adoption). To satisfy the purpose of the statute, the decision should have been the same in all situations. But the answers given by jurists varied, according to the purely legal relationship to the father, in line with decisions in other fields such as intestate succession to the father. Even more legalistic or juristic is the decision of Paul in *D.29.5.10pr:* "If a disinherited son was murdered before the inheritance of his father was accepted, the case is to be looked at according to how the facts turned out, so that if the inheritance was accepted the slaves are considered as if they belonged to someone else; but if the will has been avoided, because they would have been his if he had lived, everything is done as if he were owner."

In Roman law, an heir (under a will or on intestacy) who was neither a slave of the deceased nor a free person in the deceased's power who became *sui iuris* on his death became owner of the inheritance only when he made a formal acceptance. If he refused to accept the inheritance, the will was voided and the inheritance descended according to the rules of intestate succession. If there was an intestacy or a will and the nearest heir was a direct descendant of the deceased who became *sui iuris*, such as a son, he became heir at the moment of death (unless he abstained from the estate).

In the case decided by Paul a father died leaving a will in which he appointed an outsider to the family as heir and disinherited his son. Then the son was murdered, apparently in the paternal home. What was to happen to the slaves? Paul's opinion was that one should adopt a wait and see approach. If the heir under the will accepted the inheritance, nothing was to happen to the slaves. Their ownership was in suspense between the testator's death and the acceptance of the inheritance. If the testamentary heir refused the inheritance, the will failed, the disinherited son would be regarded as heir from the moment of the father's death, and the slaves would be treated as if they were his from that time and hence at the moment of his murder. Thus they would be questioned under torture and executed. The decision is legally irreproachable; but who but a lawyer would

reach it calmly, following out the path of legal logic without point-
ing out the brutal absurdity and the pointlessness of the slaughter of
individuals and the destruction of property? Paul's approach in no
way follows out the purpose of the *senatus consultum*, but it does
display his legal acumen.

As a final instance of the power of juristic thinking, remote from
other concerns, on this *senatus consultum* we should note that its
context in the Edict was the law of succession. With other topics it
was placed under the general rubric "Those whose testaments are
not opened," and there it was sandwiched between "If someone having passed over a will possesses an inheritance on intestacy" and
"Legacies."[25] In Justinian's *Digest,* the relevant book 29.5, headed
"*Senatus consultum Silanianum* and *Claudianum:* Those whose
testaments are not opened" lies between 29.4 "If someone having
passed over a will possesses an inheritance on intestacy or in some
other way" and 29.6 "If someone has prohibited anyone from making a will or compelled him to."[26]

Professors' approaches to law as their culture are similar, and separate illustrations need not be given here. It is not suggested that the
example of the *senatus consultum Silanianum* exhausts the subject.
All that was intended, and needed, was to indicate that jurists and
professors typically respond to legal questions not by examining the
purpose of the law or the supposed needs of the society but by using a
"legal logic" particular to their group, with little regard for the
outcome. This legal logic can vary from one society to another. Much
the same can be said of judicial responses to law as their culture,
which can also vary from one society to another,[27] and only one
example will be given here, also from slave law but this time from
Virginia in 1827.

In *Commonwealth* v. *Turner* 26 Va. (5 Rand) 678 the general
court decided that it was not a crime for an owner to beat his slave
with "certain rods, whips and sticks" "wilfully and maliciously, vio-
lently, cruelly, immoderately and excessively," if the slave did not
die. Dade, J. gave the opinion of the court: "In coming to a decision
upon this delicate and important question, the Court has considered

it to be its duty to ascertain, not what may be expedient, or morally, or politically right in relation to this matter, but what is the law." Dade went on to disclaim a "latitudinous doctrine" of lawmaking. Thus, though the lawmaking powers of common law judges were well understood, the court denied them.

> It is said to be the boast of the common law, that it continually conforms itself to the ever-changing condition of society. But, this conformity keeps on *pari passu* with those changes. Like them it is slow and imperceptible: so that society may easily conform itself to the law. When great changes take place in the social order, a stronger hand, that of the Legislature, must be applied. Thus, when slavery, a wholly new condition, was introduced, the common law could not operate on it. The rules were to be established, either by the positive enactments of the law-making power, or to be deduced from the Codes of other countries, where that condition of man was tolerated.

The only sources of law available to the court when a new social institution is introduced, Dade argued, are legislation and then legal rules from countries where that institution once existed or now exists. This second reported source is surprising. First, no foreign system is a source of law if (as is the case here) it was not accepted as authoritative. Second, for the court to borrow in this way would be for it to make law. Third, this would all the more be the case when, as would be entirely possible, the foreign systems had different rules. Dade said:

> To descend from these preliminary principles to the case in hand, it seems reasonable to suppose, that when slavery was introduced into the then English Colony of Virginia, without reference to the common law of England, which had never acknowledged it, (for villenage is not the prototype of slavery, as it has always existed here) without the positive enactments of the Parliament of the Mother Country, or of the Colonial Legislature, but at the mere will of the buyers and sellers, the condition of the slave was that of uncontrolled and unlimited subjection to the will of the master: or, it was to be modified by the established usages of those countries, where to a great extent it still prevailed, or of those extinct nations, where it had existed, and had been

subjected to well-settled and established rules; the customs of the former were but little known to a people with whom, from the influence of political and religious prejudices, they had scarcely any intercourse.

The implication of the first part of this passage is that English common law was not relevant to American slavery. If that analysis is correct, Dade seems to be arguing that since colonial slavery did not derive from English villenage, no arguments could be drawn by analogy from villenage. Even more artificial is the argument relating to foreign systems, ancient and modern: in the early days of Virginia slavery, the laws of other modern systems were scarcely known, hence "the few and vague rules" that might have restricted masters' powers must have been taken from ancient systems and the pattern of borrowing from Jewish, Greek, and Roman laws could be continued.

Dade subsequently asserts that any argument from villenage would in any event not have made a master's beating his slave a crime. We need not continue further with the court's arguments against considering beating a slave a crime, but Dade concludes:

It is greatly to be deplored that an offense so odious and revolting as this, should exist to the reproach of humanity. Whether it may be wiser to correct it by legislative enactments, or leave it to the tribunal of public opinion, which will not fail to award to the offenders its deep and solemn reprobation, is a question of great delicacy and doubt. This Court has little hesitation in saying that the power of correction does not belong to it: and, with but one dissenting voice, it declares, that it has not jurisdiction over this offense, and that the demurrer to the Indictment must be sustained.

From the dissenting opinion of Brockenbrough, J. we need note only:

It is true, that to the common law, slavery, except in the modified form of villenage, was unknown. But, the relations of superior and inferior, had their rules well established by that law. A master had the power to correct his servant; a parent, his child; and a tutor, his pupil; but the moment either of these persons transcended the bounds of due moder-

ation, he was amenable to the law of the land, and might be pros-
ecuted for the abuse of his authority, for his cruelty and inhumanity.
When slaves were introduced, although the power conferred on the
master by that relation, was much greater than that conferred by either of the others, yet the common law would easily adapt itself to this
new relation.

Thus, for this judge, a proper course was to argue by analogy from
other branches of the common law. He ends with a policy argument:

> I have not thought it necessary to say any thing on the subject of the
> consequences of the doctrine which I have supported. I do not believe,
> that in those consequences any thing can be discerned injurious to the
> peace of society. When it is recollected, that our Courts and Juries are
> composed of men who, for the most part, are masters, I cannot con-
> ceive that any injury can accrue to the rights and interests of that class
> of the community. And with respect to the slaves, whilst kindness and
> humane treatment are calculated to render them contented and happy,
> is there no danger that oppression and tyranny, against which there is
> no redress, may drive them to despair?

It is not my claim that no other societal factors entered into the
judgment or the dissenting opinion. What is important is the nature
of the judicial arguments that the judges cannot make law and that
they can look at (with a view to borrowing) ancient Jewish, Greek,
and Roman law but not at French or Spanish colonial law, and the
dissenting opinion that the common law can develop by using anal-
ogies from other parts of the system. The real issue is hidden below
the surface. How should Virginia judges, in the absence of relevant
statute, develop a law of slavery, thus, in fact, make law? The dissenting opinion is that such law should be created by analogy from
common law materials. The court's view, hidden in the wording of
Dade, is that one should borrow from Roman law. Dade in effect
excludes analogy from other branches of the common law, contemporary legal systems that accepted slavery, and he relies on ancient
systems of which only Roman law had well-developed rules that
were widely known. In 1854 the famous Harvard law professor
Luther S. Cushing wrote of the enduring significance of Roman law:

Its diffusion, from the middle ages to the present day, has taken place upon the simple principle, equally operative at this moment, that wherever, and whenever, and as to whatever, there was any want of its principles, for the regulation of human affairs, its authority has been at one recognized, admitted, and applied. An example of the Roman law occurs with reference to the institution of domestic slavery in this country. Wherever that relation has been introduced, it has been followed and regulated, in the absence of other legislation, by the principles of the Roman law.[28]

This may seem to be an exaggeration (though one should note the qualification "in the absence of other legislation"), but it does represent what the court was doing in *Commonwealth* v. *Turner*.

Because of the way these sources of law habitually come into being—they are required because of the government's disinterest in making legal rules, yet they come about by default—they seldom keep the law up to date or impart clarity to it.[29] How could one expect them to, when their creators have not been given lawmaking powers? When jurists or professors disagree, as they frequently do, how is one to decide who is giving the correct answer when none has been granted the power to give any authoritative answer, and when, therefore, there is no correct answer? In time a hierarchy of jurists or professors may emerge, but when (as is usually the case) no such hierarchy is formally established, certainty of rule or result is still not fixed. A different situation exists when judges assume the lawmaking role. In this case there is a hierarchy of judges. But certainty of law still does not result. Perhaps oddly (but an explanation is at hand), precisely in those countries where precedent is binding, judges do not set out the legal rule that in their opinion is the basis for their judgment. In both England and the United States the binding feature of a precedent is said to be the *ratio decidendi* or holding of the case, but no method of determining what is the *ratio* or holding has been found acceptable.

Jurist and law professor can, in that role, seldom hope or even wish to make a big impact on law in practice. There is one way they might do so: by encouraging legislation. But here they would be stepping out of their role. It is not by chance that the legal person-

alities known to have gotten major legislation through for their masters—Tribonian for Justinian, Henricus Coccejus for Frederick the
Great, Portalis, Tronchet, and Bigot-Préameneu for Napoleon—are
not thought of as great jurists.[30] (American law professors are in a
different category; they will not be discussed here.) Thus the legal
doctrines of jurists and professors are not geared toward immediate
practical ends. I can think of not one single legal proposition that a
Roman jurist urges because it would be useful, just, moral, or economically efficient. The situation for judges is again different. When
they are lawmakers, they are confined to the legal norm regarded as
inherent in the decision on the particular facts of the case in front of
them. They, too, can scarcely hope to make a big impact in practice,
with the sole exception in the history of the Western world of U.S.
Supreme Court justices. And just as jurists are little interested in
influencing legislation, so judges are typically—except in the contemporary United States—not concerned with such results.

These lawyers are from an intellectual culture that determines the
sources of inspiration that are accessible and acceptable. One must
emphasize that borrowing is the most fruitful means of legal change.
One may borrow from within one's own system by analogy or from
another system that has high prestige. Here, too, the borrowing may
be by analogy from a very different part of the foreign system or be of
the same rule in the same context, with or without modification. The
impact of this culture is often not realized and frequently not made
express.

Consequently, when considering any legal change or any aspect
of law and society one must always be mindful of the role of government and of these subordinate lawmakers, and one must interpret
any legislation, judicial decision, or doctrinal writing in the context
of the legal culture. In this way, and only in this way, may one come
to a true understanding.

None of the foregoing should be taken as meaning that societal
concerns have no impact on legal growth. Of course they have, but
the impact is muted and is made through the sources of law: legislation, juristic and professorial opinion, and judicial decision. Organized pressure groups can operate powerfully only on the making of

legislation, not on the other sources of law. And only legislation need not justify changes in the substance of law by means of arguments based on the legal culture. Among the sources of law, legislation is special in that as the government's source of law it can override all others, it may be least tied to the legal tradition, and it has the strength to be both radical and comprehensive. But legislation usually passes through the hands of draftsmen who are elite lawyers and thus also partake of the legal culture.

I am not claiming that there is nothing political in the opinions of jurists and professors and in judicial precedents. Of course there is.[31] Just as much of legislation on private and criminal law is nonpolitical in the sense that the legislature is not concerned to put forward particular political or social doctrines, so much of the law made in the other ways is influenced by the political perspective of the makers. This is especially true of judge-made law because judges are usually appointees of governments. But the striking feature of law made by jurists, professors, and judges remains the enormous impact of the legal tradition and culture.

The formation of Justinian's *Corpus Juris* in the sixth century, mainly from much earlier Roman material, and its subsequent history superbly illustrate the arguments in this chapter. But it is merely one example, if the most obvious. The *Corpus Juris* plays an important role in subsequent chapters and will not be discussed further here. To show that the *Corpus Juris* was not unique in its formation and subsequent history we should now turn elsewhere. Many of the arguments adduced in this chapter are also strikingly confirmed by the medieval *Libri Feudorum*, "The Books of the Feus," which in their own field of feudal law were almost as significant for development as was Justinian's *Corpus Juris Civilis* for private law in general. Eight relevant points may be made.

First, though they do contain some imperial legislation, they were a private work by Obertus de Orto, who was a judge of the imperial court of Milan. Their very success is testimony to the absence of much governmental lawmaking, by legislation, in this area. Subsequent major legislation would have supplanted them. They appear to have been composed primarily in Milan in the first half of the twelfth century. A second version contained some expressly quoted legislation and the constitutions of 1154 and 1158 of Emperor Frederick I. A third version was completed by the celebrated Bolognese jurist Hugolinus in 1233.

Second, that the *Libri Feudorum* do contain or report some imperial legislation[32] shows that the reason for the general absence of legislation is not that there could be none. Governments were insufficiently interested. Rulers had better things to do. It is not easy to determine the extent of statute law in the *Libri Feudorum* for statutory provisions may be included without being expressly mentioned. Again the most frequent source of statutes referred to is the old collections of Lombard law from the seventh and eighth centuries, which were meant for very different social conditions.

Third, a failure to accept that governments are uninterested in lawmaking has led learned men—who ought to know better—to make fundamental mistakes. Thus the splendid Scot Thomas Craig says in his *Jus Feudale,* which was first published in 1655 though written much earlier (Craig died in 1608), at 1.6.7:

> But it may seem a surprise, since the authors of these books were private men and attorneys (however great intellectually, and leaders in their own assembly), how it could come about that their opinions were not only treated as if they were statutes, but even caused imperial and pontifical laws to be subordinate to them, and took to themselves supremacy of law in their own field; since it is certain that only the pope and emperor (in the term emperor I include all rulers who recognize no superior) have the right and power of laying down the law.

And he reminds us that even the great Roman jurists, Ulpian, Scaevola, and Paul, had their authority not from their eminence but from the Emperor Justinian's approval and decree. And he goes on at 1.6.8:

> But the solution of this problem is easy. For the *Digest* received its authority not from the authors themselves but from the day of the constitution promulgated by Justinian, which is prefixed to the *Pandects,* namely the 24th December, 533 A.D. . . . . Likewise it should be considered in the case of the *Libri Feudorum* that, plausibly, they

received their authority not from Gerardus nor from Obertus [the reputed authors] but from imperial constitutions. One might reasonably believe that when these were founded on and produced in the Lombard courts, Gerardus and Obertus set down in brief notes the extent of their use and observance.

Thus, he continues, the *Libri Feudorum* were a product of imperial statute, a select digest of laws of such emperors as Lothair, Conrad, and Frederick. Craig is deceived, of course, but he was a victim of self-deception, and a very willing victim at that. For his purpose it was enough that the *Libri Feudorum* had authority: he did not have to specify the origin of that authority, especially since his main subject was Scots law (and Scotland never came under the rule of imperial legislation). He was also too good a historian not to be aware— as, indeed, he makes plain—that there was no evidence that the *Libri Feudorum* were a digest of imperial law. But he believed—and this alone can explain his approach—that such authoritative works must, of necessity, be based on direct governmental lawmaking, imperial legislation. Incidentally, he was too good a lawyer to have failed to notice that the parallel he draws with the *Digest* is no parallel. The writings of the jurists contained in the *Digest* became authoritative because—and at the time when—the *Digest* was enacted as statute. That is very different from saying the *Libri Feudorum* had authority because they contained a summary of legislation. A private work cannot be said to be authoritative because it paraphrases, summarizes, or reports legislation.

Fourth, the success of the *Libri Feudorum* is another instance of massive reception of legal transplants. They were treated as having considerable authority for the law not just in Lombardy but elsewhere as in France, Germany, the Netherlands, and Scotland. A remark of G. L. Boehmer (1715–97) in his *Principia Iuris Feudalis* published at Göttingen, where Boehmer was an illustrious professor, a subject both of the king of Great Britain and of the elector of Saxony, is instructive: "The *sources* of *common* German feudal law are the *feudal* law *of the Lombards* received throughout Germany; universal *German feudal customs;* the *common law of the empire* contained in imperial sanctions, in Roman and in canon law."[33] Thus the *Libri Feudorum* are given pride of place among the sources of feudal law common to all Germany.

But if the *Libri Feudorum* were widely received, they were greatly infiltrated by the law in the *Corpus Juris*. The accepted rule was that when the *Libri Feudorum* did not provide an answer, recourse was to be had to the *Corpus Juris* and to common law.[34] But the converse did not apply. Arguments drawn from the *Digest* and the *Code* abound in commentaries on the *Libri Feudorum,* as do references to famous scholars of Roman law. Roman categories and classifications are treated as important and to be drawn upon. To give an example from a very basic level, Henricus Zoesius (1571–1627) in his *Praelectiones Feudales* (first published in 1641), "Lectures on the Feudal Law" given at Louvain in 1623, asked whether the feu should be classified among the nominate or the innominate contracts and then whether it should be classified among the *contractus bonae fidei,* contracts of good faith.[35] The notions of nominate contracts, innominate contracts, and contracts of good faith come from discussions on Roman law.

Fifth, feudal law lasted as an important legal system long after the demise of feudalism as a meaningful social system. Thus many scholars see feudalism ending as a social system in the twelfth century, the time when the *Libri Feudorum* were being written;[36] others place its end in the later thirteenth century.[37] What is sometimes seen as a continuation of feudal society should rather be regarded as a survival of feudal law, above all of land tenure but with the recipient obliged to pay money. Yet the work of J. L. Boehmer ran at least eight editions and was last published in 1819. Thomas Craig's *Ius Feudale*, written in the very early seventeenth century, was published in 1655 and republished in Leipzig in 1716 and again in Edinburgh in 1732. The Prussian Henricus Coccejus's (1644–1719) *Juris Feudalis Hypomnemata* had four editions and was last published in Utrecht in 1747. Petrus Gudelinus's (1550–1619) *De Iure feudorum Commentarius* was first published in Louvain in 1624. Sam Stryk's (1640–1710) *Examen Juris Feudalis* appeared in numerous editions, probably the last at Vienna, undated but of 1750 or later.

And so it goes. In France, feudal law was abolished by the Revolution.[38]

Sixth, the primary lawmakers here were professors. This is so not only with regard to the authorship of the *Libri Feudorum* but also with regard to their subsequent history. Even before the third version, an *apparatus* was produced by Pillius, which was used by Accursius, who produced a standard *Glossa* for it as for the *Corpus Juris*. It remained for Hugolinus, who produced the third version, to add it, with its gloss, to the traditional arrangement of the *Corpus Juris* in the fifth volume, the *Volumen Parvum,* where it is placed after the *Authenticae*. Thereafter its fate was tied up with the *Corpus Juris* and it was regarded as part of the learned law. Many jurists, including Baldus, Bartolus, Duarenus, Hotman, Cujas, Zasius, and Paulus de Castro, who are celebrated for their work on Roman law, also contributed important writings on the *Libri Feudorum*. Cujas, indeed, produced a new arrangement, dividing the *Libri Feudorum* into five books instead of the traditional three.

Seventh, the professors were the main cause of the territorial expansion of the realm of the *Libri Feudales,* just as they were for the development of the law. Thus it is not surprising that the great Hermann Conring claimed in his *De origine juris Germanici* of 1643 that these feudal customs were transported into Germany in the fifteenth century, when law was first taught and universities were founded.[39] But, of course, the feudal system and feudal customs had existed long before. Conring says: "For the Goths, Vandals, Alemanni, Franks, Burgundians, Angles, Saxons, all the German nations who occupied by war the richest parts of the Roman Empire, each had their own laws or customs on feus no less than had the Lombards." And Conring's view found favor.[40]

The justification for the authority of the *Libri Feudorum* was the subject of much doubt, though the authority itself was not. For some, it had the same authority as the other *Libri Iuris Civilis*. Where local statute or local custom was lacking, the *Libri Feudales* prevailed.[41] Others thought the *Libri Feudales* had the force of statute as if they had been approved by the emperors and incorporated into the *Corpus Juris*.[42] Or, "By being received; that is, insofar as by a certain spontaneous decision, they were brought into the schools with the knowledge of the emperor who does not oppose the fact, and explicated and validated by the common observance of judgments."[43] Others insisted that the work was private, approved by no public authority of prince or people, and maintained that private writings did not make law. On that view, the *Libri Feudorum* do not exceed the authority of custom.[44] This confusion as to the source of authority of the *Libri Feudorum* testifies to the lack of interest on the part of the governments as to who makes the law or how it is made. The authority exists by default.

Eighth, these lawmakers saw law in part, I maintain, as their culture. Part of the traditional culture of these learned lawyers was the *Institutes* of Justinian, which had an enormous impact, for instance, on the structure of many later books dealing with local law.[45] So powerful was this tradition that we find the structure of the *Institutes* even where it was entirely inappropriate, even in feudal law, as in Sam Stryk's *Examen Juris Feudalis*.[46]

2

SLAVE LAW AND

MANUMISSION AT ROME

Roman private law so far as it concerns slaves or relates to slavery conforms very closely to the picture of legal growth portrayed in the first chapter. There was almost no legislative involvement, and there was scarcely a private law of slavery.[1] Legally slaves were property. They had no rights. But it was recognized that they were property of a very special kind. For some purposes a slave was regarded by the law as if he were a human being, for other purposes as if he were a thing. Thus the jurist Gaius in his *Institutes* (written about 161 A.D.)[2] deals extensively with slaves in book 1 (at sections 9 to 54), which concerns the law of persons, and in book 2 (at sections 13, 14a, 18 to 26, etc.), which concerns the law of things. When the slave was treated as a person, the law relating to him was more or less identical with that relating to some other group of persons, notably sons under parental authority. When the slave was treated as a thing, his position was more or less identical with that of some other animals, particularly those important beasts which were classified as *res mancipi* such as horses or cattle. As a result, one can scarcely even say that there was any particular law of slavery. This is remarkable since ancient Rome, along with the American South and parts of Latin America, is one of the tiny group of societies which in the course of human history has made considerable use of slave labor. Though it is notoriously difficult to estimate population numbers for the ancient world, the judgment of the best authorities is that slaves totaled between 35 and 40 percent of the population of the Roman world at the end of the first century B.C. At the height of slavery in the American South slaves made up about one-third of the population.[3] Moreover, in contrast to the American South, for example, Roman slaves frequently were highly educated. They might be medical practitioners—most of the doctors at Rome were slaves or freedmen—serve as bankers, ship captains, or general business agents for their masters, run businesses (even having hundreds of other slaves under their control), be highly prized gladiators or actors, or be house servants or work as field hands.

The slave presence was considerable as early as the Twelve Tables, the code of law dating from around the middle of the fifth century B.C. During the last two centuries of the republic, when Roman law most developed, Rome was, in Marxist terms, a slave society. So it continued to be during the classical period, which ended in 235 A.D. with the death of Alexander Severus, during the period of anarchy and economic ruin that followed, as well as when stability was restored under Diocletian (284–304) and when Constantine (306–37) removed the center of government to Constantinople and throughout the Christian era, until Roman law was codified under Justinian.

Only regarding manumission is there a specific body of law relating to slaves,[4] and it is probably proper to see manumission or emancipation as the central issue in the social institution of slavery (after perhaps that of who are the slaves). Can a master free slaves? If so, are there restrictions, for instance, on the numbers who can be freed, on acceptable reasons for manumission, or on manumission by will? Do freed slaves have a right to reside in the state in which they are freed? If so, do they become citizens? And, if they do, is their legal status in any way inferior to that of freeborn citizens? If it is, is the legal status of their freeborn children inferior to that of other freeborn persons?

Roman law was very tolerant of manumissions, and they were common. Slaves who were freed in one of the proper ways became Roman citizens.[5] Though they had not quite the public law rights of freeborn citizens, their freeborn children did.[6] Manumission could be *inter vivos* or by will. Restrictions on manumission were few. Naturally, manumission to defraud creditors was void,[7] and Augustus in 2 B.C. introduced restrictions on the numbers who could

be freed by will—only by will[8]—and in 4 A.D. on the age at manumission of owner and slave. Justinian abolished the restriction on
the numbers who could be freed by will.[9] In the Roman setting these
rules were reasonable enough. The primary purpose of slavery is to
maximize the benefits for the owners while minimizing the risks to
them, which requires a mixture of carrots and sticks. And manumission (with citizenship) is the juiciest carrot. As I have said, Roman
slaves could be highly skilled and earn much money for their masters. Slaves might be of any racial or national type (Rome[10] and her
allies only excepted), including some whose culture was highly regarded: other Italian peoples, Greeks, Jews, Britons, Syrians, Germans, North Africans, black Africans (relatively few), Gauls, and so
on. Hence there was no obstacle to manumission on the grounds
that slaves were of an inherently inferior racial stock.

Slaves could own no property—neither could sons or daughters
as long as their father (or grandfather) was alive—but they, like
sons, were frequently given a fund called the *peculium,* which technically belonged to their owner but which they could use as their
own within the limits laid down by the master.[11] And it was common, though not legally required, for masters to allow slaves to buy
their freedom with the *peculium,* at whatever price the master fixed.
The incentive for slaves to work hard and increase the *peculium* is
obvious. It is easy to imagine the system in operation: for instance,
the master sets the slave to trade, or work as a doctor, or perform as
an actor, on the basis that, say, 5 percent of the profit remained in
the slave's *peculium* and that the master would free him when the
slave paid him a specified sum from the *peculium.* That sum would
often be the value of the slave. The owner was not bound by the
arrangement—he could even take away the *peculium* at any time—
but there were obvious advantages for him.[12] Indeed, there is no
sign in any text, lay or legal, of a master unjustifiably taking away a
slave's *peculium* (except to defraud creditors). An owner might even
allow a slave to go where he pleased on condition only that he give
the owner a fixed sum of money annually;[13] any remaining would
go into the *peculium.*

Texts show how this system of manumission could operate. Thus, *D*.40.1.6:

> A slave had bargained money for his freedom and had given the money to his owner. The owner died before he manumitted him, and by his will he ordered the slave to be free and gave him a legacy of his *peculium*. He [Servius or Alfenus] asked whether the heirs of the patron ought to return the money he had given his owner on account of freedom. He replied if the owner, after receiving the money, had entered it in his accounts it immediately ceased to be part of the *peculium*. But if, in the meantime, until he freed him, he registered the money as due to the slave, it seemed part of the *peculium* and the heirs ought to return the money to the freed slave.[14]

The text is illuminating: it goes back to the jurist Alfenus Varus, in the first century B.C., and was still relevant in sixth-century A.D. Byzantium. The bargain between the slave and the owner had no legal force because there could be no contract between the *paterfamilias* and someone in his power. Thus the slave did not become entitled by law to his freedom when he gave the money to his owner. In any event, the money already was his owner's. But the slave was freed by his owner's will and, as frequently, he was given a legacy of his *peculium*. What was to be the fate of the money the slave had given to the owner? The answer would depend on the state of mind of the owner. How much money was in the *peculium* would depend primarily on the intention of the owner. Thus, in the present instance, if the owner treated the money he received as no longer in the slave's *peculium,* it ceased to be so; otherwise it was due under the legacy.

But that emancipation was legally permitted does not mean, of course, that all slaves were freed or even that all categories of slaves had equal chances of manumission. One may assume that field hands who worked in gangs had little chance of seeing freedom. The slaves who were likely to be freed were those whose work was valuable and who could be persuaded to work harder for the prospect of freedom. Household slaves, who interacted with the owner, would have to show themselves in the best possible light as faithful, hard-working, and amiable and might reap the benefit of freedom. Slave mistresses and children born to slaves when the father was the owner or the owner's son were often freed.[15] The legal sources indicate that slave mistresses and their children by the owner were commonplace. In one will no relationships are spelled out, but the testator, who disinherited all those who would be his heirs on intestacy, gave freedom to his slave women, Marcella and Cleopatra, and made them his heirs in equal shares. He adds that if Marcella should predecease him, her share is to go to Sarapio, Socrates, and Longus; if Cleopatra should predecease, her share is to go to Nilus. These four males are not further described, but they seem to be free. The arrangement is odd at first sight and makes sense only if the first three males are the children of Marcella, the other the child of Cleopatra. But then why are the males free and the women slaves? The only plausible answer is that the testator was the father and had freed his sons and is by his will freeing their mothers.[16]

An interesting insight into both who might be a candidate for manumission and also who the Roman state thought should be given special consideration comes from those slaves whom, by way of exception, an owner under age twenty was allowed to free by the statute *lex Aelia Sentia* of Augustus of 4 A.D.:

> J.1.6.4. By the same *lex Aelia Sentia* a master under twenty is not permitted to manumit except by court proceedings[17] after good cause for the manumission has been approved by a council. 5. Good causes for manumission are, for example, if one is manumitting one's natural father or mother, son or daughter, brother or sister, or one's teacher, nurse, or the person who brought one up, foster brother or foster sister, or someone suckled at the same breast, or a slave in order to have him as one's general agent, or a slave woman in order to marry her, provided, however, she is taken as wife within six months unless a good reason prevents this: and the master manumitting to have a procurator must not be less than seventeen.[18]

Similar reasons are adduced for allowing slaves under age thirty to be freed and given citizenship.[19]

Likewise instructive are the cases which by the time of Justinian gave rise to tacit manumission. Thus if an owner in his will appointed his slave as his heir or made him a tutor (guardian) to his children, and did not mention freedom, the slave became free.[20] If an owner who had no wife made his slave woman his concubine and intended to keep her as such until his death, the slave woman became free, and any children she conceived with her master were treated as freeborn and given the benefit of their *peculia*.[21] Manumission, sometimes on a grand scale, might also occur because of an individual owner's moral or religious convictions.

In these circumstances, it was to be expected that owners would frequently go beyond giving slaves freedom and would provide them with means to live on or would set them up in business. We have already seen a will in which an owner freed two slaves and bequeathed his entire estate to them. It was common in wills, as the legal texts show, for a slave both to be freed and made heir. A whole title (or chapter) of Justinian's *Digest,* 33.8, is devoted to the topic of legacies of the *peculium*. Most of these texts concern the *peculium* of a slave, not of a son.[22] Justinian, in the *Institutes* 4.7 *pr.,* about to deal with actions regarding the *peculium* and other actions on the dealings of sons and slaves, says that the law is much the same with regard to both and so for the sake of brevity he will focus on slaves and owners.

There was, however, a different side to manumission. Dionysius of Halicarnassus (who lived at Rome for many years after 30 B.C.), discussing the justice and decency of early Rome, digresses and contrasts the situation in his own time (in his *Roman Antiquities,* 4.24.4–25.1):

> This, however, is not the case in our day, but things have come to such a state of confusion and the noble traditions of the Roman commonwealth have become so debased and sullied, that some [slaves] who have made a fortune by robbery, housebreaking, prostitution, and every other base means, purchase their freedom with the money so acquired and straightway are Romans. Others, who have been confidants and accomplices of their masters in poisonings, murders, and in crimes against the gods or the state, receive from them this favor as their reward. Some are freed in order that, when they have received the

monthly allowance of corn given by the public or some other largesse distributed by the men in power to the poor among the citizens, they may bring it to those who granted them their freedom. And others owe their freedom to the levity of their masters and to their vain thirst of popularity. I, at any rate, know of some who have allowed all their slaves to be freed after their death, in order that they might be called good men when they were dead and that many people might follow their biers wearing their liberty-caps; indeed, some of those taking part in these processions, as one might have heard from those who knew, have been malefactors just out of jail, who had committed crimes deserving of a thousand deaths. Most people, nevertheless, as they look upon these stains that can scarce be washed away from the city, are grieved and condemn the custom, looking upon it as unseemly that a dominant city which aspires to rule the whole world should make such men citizens.[23]

The proportion of slaves so freed compared with those emancipated for good cause probably was small but cannot be estimated. What matters and justifies the long quotation is that the theme that unrestricted manumission causes crime will run through this book and is one of the standard arguments for restricting manumission.

Three forms of manumission in the late republic gave liberty and citizenship. Although they played no direct part in the subsequent unfolding of the law, they illustrate an integral part of the thesis. *Manumissio vindicta,* manumission by staff, was a juristic dodge, a fictional use of the *vindicatio in libertatem,* the "claim of freedom," which was brought when a free man was wrongfully held as a slave. A master who wished to free a slave arranged for a friend to bring the *vindicatio in libertatem* against him. The owner put up no defense, and the magistrate in charge of the hearing declared that the slave was free. The procedure needed the cooperation of the magistrate, but the initiative for this mode of manumission obviously came from individual citizens who wanted to free their slaves. The state acquiesced.

An earlier mode was *manumissio censu,* manumission by enrollment on the census. When the census was taken (once every five years when it was taken regularly), the slave, with his owner's consent, entered himself on the census list as a citizen, and this status was accepted by the censor. The census was more or less abandoned after 166 B.C. This form of manumission was probably rare even then, and the surviving evidence does not reveal whether the censor openly declared that the former slave was now a citizen. But of more relevance is that this mode of manumission also depended on the initiative of owners to free slaves with the acquiescence of the state. The owner simply declared the slave free, and the censor recorded him as such. *Manumissio censu* was not an invention of the government.

The third mode, manumission by will, is similar in this regard. Though in early Rome there was public involvement in will-making, there was no statute or official decree declaring that slaves could be freed by will. Instead, masters simply declared slaves free in their wills, the state acquiesced, and the result was achieved.

But the Roman state's acquiescence in manumission was not passive but active. The state was involved. The *manumissio vindicta* took place in front of, and by decision of, the praetor, the second highest elected public official. *Manumissio censu* needed the cooperation of the censor. And Roman wills in early days had to be approved by an assembly of the Roman people, whose approval was technically an act of legislation.

Manumission is the one part of Roman slave law that contains private law specifically concerning slaves. For political, social, and economic reasons, slavery was extremely important in Roman society. And yet in the republic and the classical period the government took no initiative to set up law permitting manumission but merely acquiesced and did almost nothing to restrict owners who wished to free slaves. Roman society could be and was greatly changed by the presence of enormous numbers of freedmen and their descendants. One could scarcely hope for a more revealing example of governmental disinterest in the making of private law. And yet Roman law is famous for its vitality.

Roman citizenship (which was given to slaves on manumission) was a highly prized commodity. For example, a decree of the senate of 177 B.C. was intended to prevent a dodge whereby citizens of other Latin states would give themselves as slaves to Romans so that they could be freed and thereby become Romans.[24] Rome's Italian allies revolted in 91 B.C. precisely because they were not given the right to Roman citizenship.[25]

By the time of Justinian there were many ways to free a slave. Manumission could be by letter provided it was witnessed by five witnesses,[26] or before friends provided the owner formally recorded the act and evidence was signed by five witnesses and the equivalent of a notary.[27] Slaves who, at the order of the owner or his heir, stood around the owner's funeral couch or walked in the funeral procession wearing the cap of liberty (*pilleus*) also became free.[28] So did a slave whose master put a notification into the official records that the slave was his son.[29] Even earlier, as soon as the empire became Christian, manumission in church bestowed freedom.[30]

Roman slaves had no legal personality, hence they could not be parties to civil lawsuits. Their use as witnesses in civil cases was restricted, but the details of the rules are not always clear. They could not give evidence against their owners, but they could give evidence regarding their own acts such as contract or the extent of an inheritance or who was their owner. But in all circumstances in which slaves were competent witnesses they had to be tortured before they were allowed to give evidence.[31] Thus, because slaves could not testify against their owners, the texts relating to their evidence on contracts they made concern instances when the owner was plaintiff and to substantiate his case he had his slaves tortured so they could give evidence for him.

Slaves could not be accusers in criminal causes, but they could be defendants. The basic proposition for a criminal action must be that, when the defendant was a slave, the same procedure was followed as for free persons.[32] But there were exceptions. Slaves could not be witnesses in criminal cases against their owners except for high treason.[33] Indeed, the first Christian emperor, Constantine, decreed that slaves or freedmen who attempted to accuse or inform against their masters or patrons would not be heard and would be crucified.[34] Later, the emperors Valens, Gratian, and Valentinian declared that no inquiry would be made when slaves accused their masters, but the slaves, along with any writing relating to the charge, would be burned.[35]

Likewise, because slaves had no legal personality, they could not marry. No marriage could exist between slaves whether of the same or different owners, and a slave could not be married to a free person.[36]

Originally, the owner's power over slaves was unlimited, but gradually some limitations were introduced to restrain the cruelty of masters. The changes can be seen in Justinian's *Institutes:*

> *J.*1.8.1 Therefore slaves are in the power of their masters. This power indeed comes from the law of nations; for we can see that among all nations alike masters have power of life and death over their slaves, and whatever is acquired through a slave is acquired for the master. 2. But nowadays, it is permitted to no one living under our rule to mistreat his slaves immoderately and without a cause known to the law. For, by a constitution of the deified Antoninus Pius, whoever kills his slave without cause is to be punished no less than one who kills the slave of another. And even excessive severity of masters is restrained by a constitution of the same emperor. For when he was consulted by certain provincial governors about those slaves who flee to a holy temple or to a statue of the emperor, he gave the ruling that if the severity of the masters seems intolerable they are compelled to sell their slaves on good terms, and the price is to be given to the owners. For it is to the advantage of the state that no one use his property badly. These are the words of the rescript sent to Aelius Marcianus: "The power of masters over their slaves should be unlimited, nor should the rights of any persons be detracted from. But it is in the interest of masters that help against savagery or hunger or intolerable injury should not be denied to those who rightly entreat for it. Investigate, therefore, the complaints of those from the family of Julius Sabinus who fled to the statue, and if you find they were more harshly treated than is fair or afflicted by shameful injury, order them to be sold so that they do not return to the power of the master. Let Sabinus know that, if he attempt to circumvent my constitution I will deal severely with his behavior."[37]

Behind the rhetoric the text seems to restrict masters' powers to inflict moderate punishment.[38]

Because slaves and freedmen could not be witnesses against their owner or former owner (except for high treason), evidence of a master's cruelty would seldom be forthcoming.[39] Indeed, the Christian emperors Valens, Gratian, and Valentinian decreed in 376 that when slaves accused their master no investigation would be made but the slaves (and any written evidence) would be burned.[40]

But if masters' powers to punish their slaves were restricted, masters' rights were protected in that no outsider, except a public official, was allowed to interfere with a slave with impunity. From the time of the early republic onward, it was murder to kill another's slave deliberately. Killing and wounding another's slave, whether deliberately or negligently, also gave the owner a civil action for damages under a statute called the *lex Aquilia*.[41] The *actio iniuriarum,* the private law action available to a free citizen for any assault on him or insult to him, was also given by an edict to an owner for attacks on his slave. The action in the ordinary case was for an invasion of the master's proprietary rights, but for serious assaults the action—though to the master—was for the attack on the slave.[42]

To avoid the possibility of confusion, it should be made explicit that to deny slaves legal personality in a slaveholding society is not necessarily to deny that slaves are human beings. To say that a slave has no legal personality is basically to deny him standing before a civil law court: he cannot be a party as either defendant or plaintiff. He is property and also a human being, and some of his human characteristics can be taken into account by law. Just as a dog, as animate property, differs from inanimate property, and legal results—such as its master's liability for damage it caused—can flow from the distinction,[43] so slaves, as thinking property, can differ from other animate property, with legal consequences such as those flowing from transactions that may at law bring benefits to the master. The slave's humanity is recognized by restraints on cruel masters. The rules may resemble those today hindering cruelty to animals in that the victim cannot sue, but they do recognize the slave's humanity since the Romans had no laws against cruelty to animals.

Because slaves could not marry, they could not bring actions for adultery with their partners.[44] But when they were manumitted, their blood relationships were taken into account, and they could not marry a real parent, sibling, or child. Indeed, they could not even marry the equivalent of a stepmother or stepdaughter.[45] And the slave's humanity could be recognized in still other ways. Thus, in the law of sale there was a rule that if a thing sold had an important physical defect that was not declared to the buyer, the buyer had for six months the possibility of suing to return the thing, that is, to redhibit, and recover the price. The jurist Ulpian records in *D.* 21.1.35: "Often on account of diseased slaves even healthy slaves are redhibited, if they cannot be separated without great difficulty or without an offense against piety. For what if they wished to retain a son and redhibit the parents? Or vice versa? And this ought to be observed both in the case of brothers and of persons joined in a settled domestic relationship."[46]

If a Roman died, whether testate or intestate, and left more than one joint heir, an action called the *actio familiae erciscundae* could be brought to divide up the estate. The judge had great discretion in deciding how the division was to be made, but the Emperor Constantine decreed, apparently in 334 A.D.: "C.3.38.11. Divisions of property should be made in such a way that close relations among slaves or serfs should remain with one single successor. For who will tolerate that children be separated from parents, sisters from brothers, wives from husbands? Therefore if people took slaves or serfs off to different legal families, they are compelled to return them together again."[47]

From a legal point of view there is no inherent contradiction in thinking of a human being as a "thing," as property,[48] but (to use Aristotle's term[49]) "thinking property." The text just quoted talks of slave husband and wife even though slave marriage had no legal validity at Rome. Such use of language is common in societies where slave marriage has no legal effect. Thus the famous *Diary from Dixie* by the South Carolinian Mary Boykin Chesnut for the years 1861 to 1865 is replete with references to slave husbands and wives and even to slave weddings.

One way a slave might show himself as thinking property was to run away. A Roman slave did not commit a crime in running away, and any punishment was left to the owner (if he recaptured the slave). A tendency to run away, however, was a defect that had to be declared to a buyer when a slave was sold.[50] But it was a serious crime to harbor a runaway[51] or support in bad faith his claim of freedom,[52] and the senate made provision to allow a person's land to be searched for runaways.[53] The state, though, made no provision for the recapturing of runaways; that was left to the initiative of private slave-catchers.[54]

It may seem odd, but is nonetheless true and must be emphasized, that even as late as Justinian's great codification in the sixth century, Christianity had made little impact on Roman private law. That is very much the case for the main themes of this chapter. Slavery remained lawful, and indeed slaves remained common. Manumission was neither made compulsory nor much easier. Masters' powers over their slaves were not reduced. In private law slaves still did not have legal personality.

But Christianity (in the guise of Constantius) decreed that Jews could not have Christian slaves.[55] Justinian went further and decreed that if a Jew, pagan, or heretic had a Christian slave, the slave would be free and the owner punished by a fine.[56] This rule was to have repercussions in the future.

A freedman had certain obligations to his former owner. The patron had rights of succession to the freedman, which varied from time to time and depended on whether the former slave died testate or intestate and had children who would otherwise be his heirs.[57] At the time of manumission a bargain might be struck that the former slave would give the patron a certain number of days' labor per year, but the amount had to be reasonable and not an imposition on his freedom.[58] More difficult to define is *obsequium*, respect. It involved, among other things, restrictions on a freedman's right to sue his patron and the obligation to support a needy patron. But the obligation of respect was also demanded from the patron. For instance, even in late law he could not be compelled to be a witness against his freedman in a criminal action, and if he failed to support a freedman in need he lost his rights of patronage.[59]

After a few hesitant beginnings it was established by Commodus, emperor from 180 to 192, that freedmen could be reenslaved for wrongs done to their patrons:

> D.25.3.6.1 This is the wording of the declaration of law of the emperor Commodus: "When it is proved that patrons are violated by the insults of their freedmen or are struck by a vilely raised hand or even are abandoned when they are laboring under poverty or illness, then first the freedmen are to be reduced to the power of their patrons and forced to perform services for their masters. But if they do not accept this warning, then they may be awarded to a purchaser by the governor and the price paid to the patrons."[60]

The rule came to be established that a freedman could not be reenslaved simply for any breach of *obsequium* but he could be for any worse form of ingratitude.[61] But a master who freed a slave because the obligation to do so was imposed upon him by a trust in a will or because the slave was "bought with his own money" (that is, money that did not form part of the *peculium* and was provided to the master by someone else) could not reenslave for ingratitude.[62]

It has been said more than once that a slave had no legal personality and hence at private law he could not sue or be sued. But what if his status was in doubt? Justinian enacted a law in 528 that stated that a person who was enslaved, but also claimed to be free, or who seemed to be free but was claimed as a slave, could appear in court on his own behalf.[63] In the latter situation, moreover, he could appear through a procurator. Even before that, in some cases when a slave was to be given his freedom directly or by a trust (*fideicommissum*), he might be given access to an official for relief. Thus, in a ruling attributed to the jurist Ulpian:

> D. 36.1.23(22).1. There is no doubt that the instituted heir may be compelled to accept and to restore the inheritance to slaves, whether they be given their liberty directly or by *fideicommissum;* for the status of the person who compels him does not entitle the heir to disregard him. The slave may even have access to the magistrate, so that one who could not yet demand his liberty left on trust nor sue for that left to him directly, may yet appear before the praetor even in his own person because of the hope for liberty and the inheritance.[64]

In general a free person who was appointed heir by will and who was not in the power of the deceased at death might refuse to become heir. But there were restrictions such as when the inheritance was left to him, as here, for trust purposes. In the present situation, the slave who cannot claim his liberty is nonetheless given direct access to the praetor.

Another very special case in which legal recognition was given to a slave's claims occurred when a person's succession rights might be affected if the deceased's widow gave birth. Elaborate precautions were laid down by law to prevent the substitution of a baby if the person whose rights might be affected believed that the widow was fraudulently claiming to be pregnant. Thus Ulpian states in *D.* 25.4.1.13:

> But even if a slave is instituted heir if no child is born, Aristo writes that the praetor has discretion to allow the slave to take some though not all of the precautions for protecting the birth. I think this view is correct: for it is in the public interest that there is no substitution of a child so that dignity of social classes and families can be preserved. Thus, where a slave of this kind has been given a chance to succeed he should be heard no matter who he is, since he is acting in his own and in the public interest.[65]

Perhaps even more significant, as we shall see in the light of subsequent developments in Spanish America, is a ruling of the "deified brothers" (Marcus Aurelius and Lucius Verus, 161–69 A.D.) reported in *D.*40.1.5 *pr.,* which says that if someone claims he had bought himself with "his own money" and was not freed he could institute proceedings against his owner on whose good faith he had reliance. The proceedings were not in the regular courts but before the prefect of the city or, if in a province, before the governor. "With his own money" means, as *D.*40.1.4.1 says, "with money not proceeding from the slave's owner," and is not to be taken as indicating that a slave could own anything. Likewise, the text does not mean that if someone, wishing to free a slave, offers to buy him, the owner must sell. Rather, if an owner accepts money to free a slave and fails to do so, the slave acquires a status permitting him to institute such proceedings.

These specific instances of legal proceedings on behalf of a slave involve situations in which the slave might have some right to freedom. But finally, we should turn to an aspect of *J.*1.8.2, a text which has already been quoted and is also reported in the *Digest,* 1.6.2. A slave who was cruelly treated, or according to the *Digest* 1.6.1, had been forced to commit some indecency or foul malpractice, could flee to a shrine or a statue of the emperor. There would then be a judicial inquiry and if the master's wrongful behavior was proved, the slave was to be sold so that he did not again return to the power of the owner. In this way, slaves, who could not bring an action, had indirect access to the courts if they were mistreated. In one particular situation however, even earlier, the emperor Hadrian had ruled that slaves would be allowed a hearing before the provincial governor if they had been castrated.[66]

One aspect of sources of law ought to be stressed at this stage. Sources of law, in the sense of factors that give legitimacy to legal rulings, not only vary from state to state but also stress different elements in the law. The most significant source of law at Rome—not necessarily quantitatively but in the sense of determining what was recorded—was juristic opinion. The jurists were not interested in analyzing (and hence reporting) minor administrative regulations, but these existed, of course, and we come upon some of them in passing.[67] We can be sure that detailed regulations, that have not come down to us, existed in the Roman Empire for behavior in markets, taverns, and so on. And we can also be sure that slave conduct would be included. For other societies, especially for English America, such control of slaves is extreme in the recorded statutes. And there did exist a very marked difference in the law of the two societies. A word of caution is needed so that the contrast is not given too much emphasis because of the sources of law. As we shall see, it was a standard requirement in English America that a proportion of persons on a plantation be white. It is only from a nonlegal source, Suetonius, *Divus Iulius,* 42, that we know that Julius Caesar enacted that on estates one-third of shepherds should be freeborn males above puberty.

The Roman law of slavery, like Roman private law in general, thus had an organic development over more than a millennium. There is a unity apparent in this legal evolution despite the changes from city-state to world empire, republican government to imperial rule, the shift of empire from Rome to Constantinople, economic changes, and the acceptance of Christianity as the official religion. But in the second quarter of the sixth century Roman law was to be given a stable form which made it accessible, if not necessarily easily accessible, to future centuries and peoples. Over the centuries a huge mass of respected juristic writings and imperial statements of the law had accumulated. In 527 Justinian became Byzantine coemperor with his uncle, Justin, and sole emperor in 528 on the latter's death. He at once began to restate the law. He started with the imperial rescripts, which had already been collected on three occasions. A stated aim was to make the law more accessible, but he also wanted the law to be updated. The finished work, Justinian's *Code,* was published in 529 and has not survived because it was replaced in 534 by a revised *Code,* and that did survive. The *Code* is in twelve books, each subdivided into titles (which are like chapters) devoted to a particular legal subject. Within each title the pronouncements of the emperors are arranged in chronological order. The work is massive and in a standard modern edition runs to almost five hundred pages of text in double columns. After the first *Code* Justinian turned his attention to the enormous surviving body of juristic writings from the first century B.C. to the third century A.D. Naturally, the jurists had made the same points over and over again, often relying on the authority of their predecessors. Equally naturally, they often contradicted one another. To settle some points of law that had been left unresolved by the jurists and had not been decided by subsequent imperial rescripts, Justinian issued the *Fifty Decisions,* which have not survived as a separate body though presumably many are included in the second *Code.* Then, in December 530, he set up a commission to collect and abridge the writings of the jurists, cutting out all repetitions and contradictions and anything that was stated elsewhere—that is, in the *Code* (and *Fifty Decisions*). The resultant *Digest* is in fifty books divided into titles, and each title contains fragments of juristic writings, each of which begins with the name of the author and the name and volume number of the original book. Within each title some slight attempt was made to arrange the fragments, but systematic ordering of materials is not a strong point of the *Digest.* The *Digest* came into force as law on 30 December 533. It is almost double the length of the *Code.*

At the same time, Justinian had ordered the preparation of an elementary textbook for students, the *Institutes,* which was modeled on a second-century textbook, the *Institutes* of Gaius. This is arranged in four books, is about one-twentieth the size of the *Digest,* and is the only part of Justinian's compilation that is reasonably well organized. It made Roman law immediately accessible, and from the eleventh century, when the Reception of Roman law can be said to have begun, until (almost) the present day, it has been the student's basic introduction to the study of law in the Western world. It came into force as statute on the same day as the *Digest.* Thus was Roman law codified and reduced to a format that made possible the subsequent Reception of Roman law. The *Code, Digest,* and *Institutes,* together with *Novellae*—Justinian's later legislation, which had little impact on the further development of Western law because the new rulings were mostly in Greek—came much later to be known as the *Corpus Juris Civilis.*[68]

3

SLAVE LAW IN SPAIN AND

SPANISH AMERICA

In the Iberian peninsula law was very largely derived from Roman law. We need go no further back than the Visigoths, and we can concentrate on the *Visigothic Code,* the famous *Liber iudiciorum* or *Liber iudicum.* The Visigoths were a Germanic tribe who penetrated inside the Roman Empire, at times allying with the Romans, at times at war with them. They left Italy, which they had ravaged, in 412 and settled in Gaul, where eventually a Visigothic kingdom was established. The Visigoths crossed the Pyrenees, and in 457 apparently a considerable number of peasant families settled in the Tierra de Campos. After defeat at the hands of the Franks at Vouillé (where the Visigothic king Alaric II was killed), the Visigoths as a whole immigrated into Spain, and eventually Leovigild (568–86) established his capital at Toledo.

The Visigoths had many Roman citizens subject to them, and Alaric II compiled for them the *Breviarium Alaricianum* or *lex Romana Visigothorum.* In that period law was personal, not territorial. Thus in the Visigothic kingdom, the Visigoths were controlled by Visigothic law, and their Roman subjects were bound by Roman law. The *Breviarium Alaricianum* therefore does not contain laws of Visigothic kings but Roman imperial rulings and writings of Roman jurists.

As this history might suggest, the Visigoths showed a keen interest in law, and indeed they were the most prolific lawmakers among the ancient Germans. Even earlier, Euric II (466–84) had issued a code or collection of laws, the *Codex Euricianus,* for his Visigothic subjects. It has long been recognized that this work, writ-

ten in Latin (which has survived only indirectly), is heavily Romanized.[1] In fact, it is so Romanized that some scholars cannot
believe it was meant for Visigoths alone.[2]

The Visigoths' crowning achievement in law is the *Visigothic
Code,* compiled and published by King Reccesvind (653–72) in
654. This massive work is in twelve books, and there is no doubt
that the predominant element of the legislation in it is Roman law
though probably deriving from the living tradition rather than from
the Byzantine *Corpus Juris Civilis.* Its subsequent history in Spain is
worth repeating.

The Visigothic era in Spain ended in 711 as a result of the Moorish
invasion, but the *Liber iudiciorum* did not vanish from sight. Law
was, of course, much localized, and customary law remained powerful. With time, in those territories and for those people to whom the
Liber iudiciorum applied, it either had its force and scope of application reduced or it had them increased.

In Septimania and Catalonia, the *Liber iudiciorum* continued in
force as the personal law of the *hispani.* Pipin declared in 769 that the
inhabitants of Aquitania should live according to their personal law,
and this was confirmed for all the *hispani* of Septimania and Catalonia
by subsequent Carolingian rulers in a number of capitularies: this personal law was Visigothic law. The capitularies did also weaken the
applicability of the *Liber iudiciorum,* because they settled questions of
political order, military service, and criminal law, but the materials of
the *Liber iudiciorum* were much used for private law. It was the most
widely used law in Catalonia in the eighth to the tenth centuries. But it
did decay with the growth of other local law. The local charters given
to recovered territory had precedence over the *Liber iudiciorum.*
Count Ramon Berenguer (1035–76) promulgated usages (usatges) to
supplement the *Liber iudiciorum,* above all with regard to feudaliza-
tion. In contracts there were frequent renunciations of the *Liber
iudiciorum,* and in 1251 the Catalan Cortes forbade its invocation.
The Mozarabs—that is, Christians living under Moorish rule—received the *Liber iudiciorum* as their personal law, and they retained it
whether they fled into Christian kingdoms as a result of the persecu-
tion in the second half of the ninth century or whether the place in
which they lived was conquered. Elsewhere, throughout the Peninsula,

there are also signs that the *Liber iudiciorum* was used: in Asturias, Galicia, northern Portugal, Navarre, and Aragon. But the deepest penetration was in Leon, where, from the tenth century, it was customary to decide lawsuits by its rules. Local *fueros* prevented it from having general force during the eleventh and twelfth centuries, but afterwards, until the reign of Alfonso IX, it was used as the law in force to cut down on appeal the judgments in the king's court and became ever more the general law of the kingdom. A similar happening occurred in Toledo.

None of the above is to be taken as suggesting that the acceptance of the *Liber iudiciorum* was anywhere complete. What was borrowed was not everywhere the same and was not everywhere to the same extent. What matters to us, though, is simply the fact that its contents were accepted in a greater or lesser degree as the law throughout the Peninsula, centuries after its promulgation, by peoples differing in many respects from the Visigoths. And its history does not stop with Alfonso IX. Ferdinand III of Castile (1230–52), the son of Alfonso IX, had the *Liber iudiciorum* officially translated into Castilian with the title of *Fuero Juzgo.* The *Fuero Juzgo* was then given, as if it were the local, individual, *fuero,* to the towns as they were conquered from the Moors: for instance, to Córdoba (1241), Cartagena (1243), Seville (1248). His son, Alfonso X (1252–84), gave the *Fuero Juzgo* as the local *fuero* on an even grander scale: to Alicante, Elche, Lorca, Murcia, and Talavera, for example. Subsequent kings continued the process.[3]

The greatest legal achievement of the Spanish Middle Ages was *Las Siete Partidas,* the enormous compilation promulgated by Alfonso X, the Wise, and its final shape was probably fixed around 1265. It was a very ambitious attempt to substitute in all Castile a new legal system, heavily inspired by Roman law, for the old local law and municipal *fueros,* which varied from place to place. The Roman law that was borrowed was that which was easily accessible in Justinian's *Corpus Juris Civilis. Las Siete Partidas* were confirmed as law in the *leyes de Toro* of 1505, as were the municipal *fueros,* including the *Fuero Juzgo.*

Slaves are mentioned frequently in the Spanish legal sources. Manumission continued. Thus, for example, the *Visigothic Code* 5.7.1. provides that if a person on the point of death frees his slaves either in writing or orally in front of witnesses, the will is valid provided that within six months it is proved by from three to five trustworthy witnesses. Likewise, gifts (or legacies) thus made to the freed slaves are valid if they are proved by oral or written evidence. As in Roman law, the *Visigothic Code* states that ingratitude on the part of a freedman was ground for reenslavement.[4] The *Visigothic Code*, presumably under the impetus of Christianity, appears to recognize the validity of slaves' marriages. Thus, in 3.2.5, King Chintasvint enacts that whoever marries his female or male slave to the slave of another without the owner's knowledge forfeits his slave and any children to the owner.[5] The impact of Christianity appears more clearly in the provisions relating to Jews, and especially for us, stating in 12.3.12 that a Jew could not have a Christian slave. This, as we have seen, was already the law at Rome. By a decretal of Pope Hadrian (from 740 A.D., which is preserved in the *Corpus Juris Canonici* in *Decretales* 4.9.1), a slave could marry even in opposition to his owner but he remained a slave.

As at Rome, slaves had no legal personality and could not be parties to a civil law action. And there were restrictions on their appearing as witnesses. When a homicide occurred among free persons and no free man was there who was not implicated, a slave who was present was allowed to testify.[6] But otherwise, the law of Chintasvint continues, slaves were not allowed to give evidence in matters of great importance, but they were in minor matters such as actions "involving title to lands, vineyards or buildings." This seems to refer to private law actions but certainty is not possible. They could also be witnesses in disputes involving themselves. In general, however, slaves were unworthy of belief unless they were known to be innocent of any crime and were not seriously oppressed by poverty. Their testimony was never allowed to contradict that of a freeman except when there had been a homicide. A slave could not accuse his master, and if a slave who was sold accused his former master, not only was the evidence inadmissible but the former owner, on paying the price, could recover and punish the slave.[7] A freedman or his descendants could not give evidence against a patron or his children, and the penalty for attempting to do so was reenslavement.[8] Freedmen could not testify except when the evidence of freeborn men was lacking. But their freeborn children could testify.[9]

The *Visigothic Code* 5.4.17 derogated from Roman law. When a slave took refuge in a church, claiming that his owner had ill-treated him, the owner could not be forced to sell the slave. The priest or custodian of the church had to return him at once, provided the owner pardoned the slave for this fault.

Slavery was regulated incompletely in some of the local *fueros*,[10] but we need not linger over these because they had no real impact on law in the New World.

Manumission appears even more prominently in *Las Siete Partidas,* which devotes title 22 of the fourth *partida* to it. Whereas Roman law had declared that slavery was contrary to natural law (but accepted by the law of nations),[11] *Las Siete Partidas* declares that by nature all creatures are free, especially humans, who have understanding above all others, and especially those of noble courage.[12] No particular legal consequence seems to flow from this fine sentiment. The master could manumit his slave in church (as in Roman law)[13] or outside or in front of a judge or elsewhere, by will or by letter. When manumission was by will the owner must be fourteen; seventeen was the age fixed by Justinian.[14] Otherwise the owner must be twenty as in Roman law. The text continues that if the slave that the master wanted to manumit was his son or his daughter or his father or mother or his brother or sister or his teacher, or the person who brought him up, or his foster child of either sex or one who had suckled at the same breast, or a slave who had saved the master from death or bad reputation, or a slave who was to act as his general agent or to receive his goods (and who was at least seventeen) or a woman slave whom he intended to marry (in which case he had to take an oath that he was freeing her for that reason and marry her within six months), then the master proving the above circumstances in front of a judge, and being less than twenty but more than seventeen, could free his slave.[15] The influence of Roman law (as set out in *J.*1.6.4) is more than obvious. Thus to isolate one example, when the owner wished to free his slave by writing or before friends, five witnesses were needed, exactly as is set out by Justinian in his *Code* at 7.3.1.1 and 7.6.2. In certain instances, too, the slave would be freed against the wishes of the master, for instance, if a slave with the knowledge of his master married a free person,[16] or if a slave with the knowledge and consent of his master became a cleric.[17] Slaves who were appointed heirs by the master in his will became free.[18] But a master could not in his will make all his slaves his heirs and free if he did not have sufficient goods to pay his debts.[19] As in the law of Justinian, if an owner in his will nominated a slave as guardian to his children, the slave would become free even without an express grant of freedom (though he would be the guardian only if he were twenty-five or reached that age).[20]

If one of the coowners of a slave appointed him his heir and freed him, and he had made him heir with the intention that he be free, the other coowner was bound to accept the price for his share. But if the coowner appointed him heir, intending that he remain a slave, the other coowner would obtain the inheritance and become full owner of the slave.[21] By *Las Siete Partidas* 4.22.1, if one of the joint owners wished to free a slave he could do so, and the others could be compelled to sell their shares to him. (In the law, the words *o otro alguo* might be interpreted to mean that even an outsider might compel the sale to him of such a slave, but this seems implausible.) A master could reenslave for ingratitude a slave whom he had freed except when he had received his price for the manumission or had freed the slave following a trust imposed on him by will.[22] Jews and Moors were forbidden to have Christian slaves.[23]

Las Siete Partidas also declared that an owner could punish a slave only in due measure[24] and could not hit him with a stone or stick or anything else that was hard. If he did but did not intend to kill his slave and the slave died, the owner was sentenced to banishment for five years. And if the master punished with the intention to kill, he was subject to the penalty for murder. In this regard, the owner of a slave is expressly placed on the same level as a father punishing his son, a teacher his pupil, or a master his free servant. A different law, 4.21.6, states that an owner has full power over his slave to do what he wants. But he must not kill the slave or treat him with savagery or strike him contrary to the reason of nature or starve him to death. Otherwise the slave can complain to a judge, and if the complaint is true the slave will be sold in such a way that he will never return to his master and the price will be given to the master. (The law gives the master the right to kill the slave for sexual intercourse with his wife, daughter, and such persons.) This provision clearly derives from the Roman text conserved in *J*.1.8.1 and *D*. 1.6.2. There is the same emphatic statement that owners have full power over their slaves, then provisions that contradict this, then the same remedy, sale of the abused slave so that he does not return to the power of the owner. There is the difference, though, that abused slaves are given direct access to the courts to make their complaint whereas the Roman ruling ordered a judicial investigation when slaves fled to a shrine or statue of the emperor and claimed to be abused. The rule of *Las Siete Partidas* perhaps represents only one small step toward giving legal personality to slaves, though Roman legal thinking was so formalistic that Roman jurists could never have taken this step.

All the gains made by a slave, such as when he received a legacy by the will of some third party, belonged to the owner. And if the owner set the slave up in business, as in a shop or ship, for example, the master was bound to fulfill the slave's contracts.[25]

The Spanish sources' attention to the law relating to slaves is not surprising because slavery continued to be a living institution in Spain though the number of slaves was small and they were almost entirely domestic servants. The impact of Justinian's *Corpus Juris Civilis* on the legislation in *Las Siete Partidas* relating to slavery is in line with its impact on *Las Siete Partidas* generally. And it must not be forgotten that the *Corpus Juris* operated for practical purposes as subsidiary law. Whenever the appropriate Spanish sources failed to give an answer to a question, recourse would be had to the *Corpus Juris* as it had been glossed and explicated by famous jurists.

Christopher Columbus's first trip to the New World, under the auspices of Ferdinand and Isabella of Castile, was in 1492. In 1493 Alexander VI, in his two papal bulls *Inter coetera,* gave the new lands "discovered and to be discovered" to Isabella and Ferdinand equally and by personal title and to their "heirs and successors, the kings of Castile and Leon." Thus these territories of the New World, when accepted by the monarchs of Castile, were incorporated into the kingdom of Castile. Medieval jurists such as Bartolus, Baldus, Mateus de Afflictis, and Azevedo unanimously held that territories of infidels which were acquired by any Christian prince would be incorporated in his existing territory through accession. *Accessio* was the mode of acquiring property in Roman law when one thing was incorporated into another. The owner of the principal thing became the owner of the combined thing.[26] Thus the territories granted to Spain in the New World became in law part of Castile and were governed by the same laws and enjoyed the same privileges.[27] Thus, there was a complete transplant of the law of Castile to the New World territories.

With this legal transplant went the Castilian law of slavery. There was thus in the New World law regulating slavery before there were slaves to be regulated except for the Indians captured by Columbus and brought back to Spain.[28] This slave law, which in Spain was already centuries old when the New World was discovered, was framed not for conditions as they existed or would exist in the Spanish colonies but for conditions in Spain. Much of it, moreover, including the law on freeing slaves, had derived in large measure from the rules of Roman law as they were set out in the compilation of Justinian. As we saw in the first chapter, the lesson of legal history teaches that law once in place is not easily replaced because governments usually have better things to do with their time than legislate on private law, and changed social circumstances do not in themselves change law. Law made for one time and for one place lives on for a very different time and a very different place.[29]

Nonetheless, legal transplants do undergo change over time in their new setting. That is true also for Castilian slave law in the New World. The point, though, is that such changes are often not far-reaching. And the law of slavery in the Spanish New World was essentially nonracist at the outset. Racism, if it came to exist in the society, would have the hard task of trying to penetrate an existing, well-developed body of law, which was made in Spain, not in the colonies.

We need not here discuss the legal and theological debate as to whether the native Indians were slaves or could be enslaved. It is enough to note that from an early date it was settled that they were free and could not be enslaved.[30] Many Negroes, though, were imported and enslaved.

There was, indeed, considerable legislation for the Spanish American territories,[31] though this was, as one would expect from the first chapter, mainly concerned with administrative matters. Still, one of the earliest provisions was in derogation of *Las Siete Partidas* 4.22.5, which provided that if a slave with the consent of the owner married a free person the slave became free. The problem in Spanish America was, of course, that Indians were free, and (if we are to believe Queen Juana) masters wishing their slaves to be protected from sin allowed them to marry Indians, and the slaves then claimed their freedom. Thus the queen on 10 July 1538 in a *Real Cédula* addressed to the viceroy and governor of New Spain declared that marriage with a free person did not bring freedom.[32] Of particular importance here is the *Recopilación de las leyes de los Reynos de las Indias* promulgated by Carlos II in 1680. Like the Castilian *Recopilaciones*, this work gathers together normative rules already promulgated which are to be treated as still in force, and the *Recopilación* gives them new legislative force. Since it was promulgated as general law, rules in it that once were restricted to a particular territory now applied everywhere. The *Recopilación* expressly provides in book 2, title 1, law 2, that whenever the relevant law was not to be found in it or in other royal decrees, the law in force was that of Castile conform to the *leyes de Toro*. By far the largest body of law sanctioned by the *leyes* was *Las Siete Partidas*. As even a glance at the index to the *Recopilación* shows, slaves and free blacks were numerous, and particular rules were made for them. But no rule in the entire collection touches on manumission or changes the law on the master's right to punish. Only incidentally do we see that slaves could still marry, since 7.5.5 (of 1527) says that slaves do not become free when they marry. (But a particular *Real Provisión,* dated from

Seville, 11 May 1526, to the Audiencia Real de las Indias resident in Hispaniola and to the governor and other judicial officials there, on the occasion of the importation of two hundred slaves, one hundred males, one hundred females, and which contains the same rule, repeats the rule of *Las Siete Partidas* that if a free person marries a slave and the owner is there or knows of it and says nothing, the slave automatically is freed and cannot be reenslaved.)[33] Naturally, there was concern for the soul of the slave. Thus, 1.1.13 (of 1538 and 1549) declares that slaves, whether blacks or mulattoes, are, like Indians, to be introduced to the holy Catholic faith. There were many police regulations. Thus, 7.5.12 forbids blacks to go at night through cities, towns, and villages outside the houses of their masters. An early humanitarian provision of 1563 in the *Recopilación* 7.5.6 enacts that when a slave is being sold the owner must give preference as buyer to the slave's Spanish father who wants to buy the slave to set him free.

Even more significant is a royal decree of 31 May 1789 dealing only with slavery, the *Real Cédula de su Magestad sobre la Educación, Trato y Occupaciones de los Esclavos, en Todos sus Dominios de Indias e Islas Filipinas, baxo las Reglas que se Expresan.*[34] A reason expressly given for its promulgation is the difficulty experienced by slaveowners in finding the relevant law in *Las Siete Partidas* and the other applicable statutes. This decree in no way changes the law on manumission. The humanity of slaves is again recognized in that their illicit sex is to be restrained and marriage encouraged, even with the slaves of other masters,[35] and that they have to be brought up in the Catholic faith.[36] Masters must provide for slaves, including supplying them and even their free children below certain ages with food and clothing,[37] and the prime occupation of slaves is declared to be agriculture, not sedentary duties.[38] On feast days of obligation the owners can neither force nor permit their slaves to work but must, after the hearing of mass, provide simple diversions for them, though the sexes are to be separated.[39] Separate quarters are to be provided for the unmarried of each sex.[40] The old and infirm who cannot work are to be maintained and cannot be freed so that the master will escape the burden.

Owners and their majordomos are given only limited rights of punishment. Depending on the nature of the offense, they may use imprisonment, shackles, clubs, or stocks (but may not hold slaves in them by the head), or beating but not exceeding twenty-five strokes, or with a gentle instrument of punishment that does not cause serious bruising or bleeding.[41] Wrongdoing by a slave that requires more serious punishment is to be remitted to government officials.[42]

Excessive punishment by the owner or majordomo is to be treated as a criminal offense with the same penalties as for injuring a free person. In addition, the slave, if possible, is to be sold to another owner; if he cannot be sold, the owner is to provide for his keep without the slave returning to him.[43] These restrictions on the master's powers are not much greater than those under Justinianian Roman law. No person other than the owner or majordomo has the right to punish slaves.[44] The difficulty of proving the excesses of a master on his slaves is specifically noted, and priests who say mass or explain Christian doctrine to slaves are to instruct themselves both by their efforts and also through the slaves as to how masters behave. And priests can file complaints to the *procurador síndico*.[45] Slaves are not given the right to make official complaints about their master's conduct.[46]

There is no doubt that Spanish American slavery was racist. Only blacks and descendants of blacks (and, in the early days, Indians) were slaves. Whites were not enslaved even when during warfare, as with the English, they were captured and taken prisoner.

The Roman law tradition taken over by Spain with minor alterations remained the law with minor alterations for the Spanish American colonies. Manumission, as at Rome and in Spain, was subject to few legal restrictions. And from an early date there was a free black population.

A very particular development that occurred in Spanish America must be stressed. By what is called *coartación* a slave who by himself or through another presented his just price to his master became free. The exact extent of *coartación* is uncertain, and whether the slave could always take the initiative in demanding that the just price be set is not entirely clear. The implication of the appropriate passage in book 1, title 5, of the most famous private law book of Spanish America, José Maria Alvarez, *Instituciones de derecho real de Castila y de Indias* (first published in 1818, republished several times thereafter), is that the slaves' right to freedom on presenting the just price was unqualified. But that, as we shall see, cannot always be wholly accurate.

The procedure is first clearly evidenced for Cuba for 1768, where it is accepted as fully existing in a *Real Cédula* of 21 June addressed to the governor of Havana. The concern of the *Cédula* is with the payment of tax (*alcabala*)—a significant point from the perspective of the general thesis of this book—on the sale of such slaves.[47] Indeed, the indirect way in which the subject of *esclavos coartados* occurs in official documents—as in the *Real Cédula* of 21 September 1769 to clarify the preceding one[48]—with the status never discussed, indicates that *coartación* resulted from practice, not from official intervention or royal legislation. Even the opinion of the Consejo de las Indias on *coartación*, dated from Madrid, 5 December 1788, in response to a question from the governor of Havana, does not cast light on the origin of the status of *esclavo coartado*. The council examined the issue of the price of slave children born to a slave mother who was *coartada*. The decision was that such slaves, although born to an *esclava coartada*, ought not on that account to be free from all the effects that slavery causes with regard to the absolute power that owners and masters should have over them. That decision meant that though the price was fixed for the mother, it was not for the children. This is justified on the basis that a different decision for Havana would open the floodgates elsewhere, that the royal right to the *alcabala* would be considerably diminished, and that in time it would result in there being many free persons. The king accepted the opinion. In this absence of direct legislation creating the status, the Spanish monarchy was in line with other governments charged with making private law: it showed little interest apart from peacekeeping and, as here, raising money.

The absence of any legislation creating the status is strikingly confirmed by Alvarez's treatment of the subject. He asserts that the authority for his statements is "by argument from" *Las Siete Partidas*

4.22.2 and the *Real Cédula* of 31 May 1789, cap. 3.[49] *Las Siete Partidas* has nothing à propos in that text but says that if one of two or more owners wishes to free the slave the others must sell to him and that in default of agreement the judge will fix the price, and then the slave will become free even in the face of opposition from the other owners. The *Cédula,* which is the royal direction on the education, treatment, and work of slaves, also has nothing à propos in chapter 3, which deals with the work to be done by slaves. After stating that the labor of slaves should be primarily in agriculture and field work and not in a sedentary occupation, from sunup to sundown, it decrees that slaves are to be given two hours in the day to be used in manufactures and work for their own benefit and advantage. Alvarez's treatment shows that *coartación* had simply grown up in practice and that he was making a valiant attempt to find authority for it.

That the field of application of *coartación* might be very restricted is shown by the extract of the *Código negro carolino* for Santo Domingo, conforming to the royal decree of 23 September 1783, and issued on 14 March 1785.[50] In chapter 22, laws 7 and 8 recognize the existence of *siervos coartados,* but other articles show that emancipation was very restricted. Chapter 19 declares that since freedom is the greatest reward for slaves, few actions are worthy of it. Chapter 19, law 1, then lists the *justas causas* of emancipation: disclosure of a conspiracy or ambush against the life of the master; disclosure of an insurrection or intended general running away; having saved a white's life in a similar situation; having stopped the spread of fire from a public building or country dwelling to the building or farm of his owner or another proprietor; having sustained with necessaries his owner and his children for a long time; having given birth to six live children who reach the age of seven years; thirty years of faithful service; for one who came from a foreign colony as a result of flight and shipwreck and who abjures the errors of heathenism and religious fellowship in which he had been instructed, with no injury to an agreement with the neighboring colony; appointment as heir or universal legatee of his owner, or as ˇestamentary executor, tutor, or curator of his children. The chapter then allows manumission for similar reasons, which are "left to the discretion of the wise hand who guides the Island of Hispaniola" and who makes good the value of the slave to the owner from the public purse in those cases when freedom does not come from the will of the owner at his own inclination. Chapter 19, law 2, declares that to avoid thefts, masters are refused the unlimited right to confer freedom simply in return for payment of the price. Chapter 19, law 3, lays down that a slave cannot proceed to liberty who does not justify in a recognized process his good conduct and behavior, and the ways in which he acquired what he offers, and that the judges cannot dispense with these requirements even at the wish of the slave's owner. And chapter 19, law 4, declares that the permission of the governor is necessary for the conferment of liberty. *Coartación* would thus seem to be permitted only when the other requirements for emancipation were fulfilled.

These restrictions on manumission in the *Código* have led distinguished scholars to misunderstand *coartación* in Santo Domingo. Even so distinguished a scholar as Hans Baade overlooked the provisions on *coartación* here and declared that the institution was not used in all parts of the Spanish Empire.[51] For David B. Davis, the existence of what he believes to be the unrestricted right of an *esclavo coartado* to get his freedom, contrasted with the severe restrictions here on owners freeing their slaves, indicates "that coartación was regarded as an unusual transaction in which a master voluntarily agreed to sell liberty to a highly superior slave."[52] Such an arrangement, though, with *coartación* often the only route to manumission, would be a positive incentive to theft and robbery had it been allowed. Moreover, it is significant that the purpose of chapter 22, laws 7 and 8, is not to regulate the main aspects of *coartación:* the possibility of *coartación* emerges indirectly from the articles.

Though Roman law did not know *coartación,* it was an easy development from Roman law. Thus *Las Siete Partidas* 4.22.2 is simply a restatement of C.7.7.1, which, though it dates from 530 A.D., has deep roots in classical law. More to the point, an owner could by will grant freedom to a slave on the performance of a condition, frequently the payment of a fixed sum of money to the heir. The heir was not allowed to do anything to impede the occurrence of the condition. As early as the middle of the fifth century B.C., the code known as the Twelve Tables enacted that if a *statuliber* (as such a slave was called) was sold by the heir, he became free on payment of that amount to the purchaser.[53] Again, a master could sell a slave on the condition that he be freed in certain circumstances, and this bargain was binding on the purchaser and his successors in title.[54] We have no text stating that the condition could be the payment of a fixed sum to the purchaser, but there is no principle that would exclude such an arrangement. That is, Roman law recognized that there could be a legal right adhering to a slave that he become free when he paid a certain sum to his owner. What Roman law did not recognize (in the absence of a duty imposed by another on the owner) was that there could be a legally binding agreement between a master and his slave, or that a slave had any right to freedom on presentation of a just price.

But there is still more to the issue. Roman law admitted, as we have seen, that if a cruelly abused slave fled to a statue of the emperor or a religious shrine there would be a judicial inquiry and on the cruelty being proved the slave would be sold so that he did not come again into the power of the owner (*J*.1.8.1; *D*.1.6.2). Spanish law in *Las Siete Partidas* 4.21.6 then took the small practical step of allowing the slave direct recourse to the courts in such circumstances, thus recognizing his legal personality to that extent. And this provision could be used in the Spanish New World.[55] Roman law recognized that the owner might allow the slave a *peculium*. The slave had no legal right to it, but in practice a master would often allow a slave to purchase his freedom with the *peculium*. We have no textual information on how the system worked, but we can guess. One obvious arrangement would be that the master fixed a price and when the slave had that amount in his *peculium* and gave it to the master, the master would free him. The master either would allow the slave to earn money outside of the house provided only that he give a daily sum to the owner, or allow him to keep a percentage of what he earned, or allow him to labor on his own account for a certain amount of time each day or each week.[56] In any event, the owner had a selfish aim (in addition possibly to some kindliness). The slave with such motivation would both be more tractable and work harder and thus benefit the owner financially. What price would the owner set? We do not know, but we can easily believe that it would be the slave's market value. The master who made such a bargain was under no legal obligation to perform, but he would have reasons for keeping the bargain. His honesty would work as an incentive for his other slaves, this slave would otherwise become difficult and irresponsible, and it cost the master nothing because he could buy a replacement. Presumably, only a small percentage of slaves would be able to earn their freedom in this way. Agricultural laborers most likely could not. Spanish law in the Americas went further. The slave could legally enforce the agreement, or take his owner to court to have a price fixed that was not exorbitant. Here was another step toward recognizing the slave as having legal personality. But how significant was the step? What does it tell one about the nature of Spanish American slavery, about racism, and about slave law in a racist society?

Before we deal with these questions, we should look at another Roman text, which appears directly relevant, *D.*40.1.5 *pr.:* "If anyone says he was bought with his own money, he can institute proceedings with his owner to whose good faith he had recourse, and complain because he is not being manumitted by him, at Rome in front of the prefect of the city, in the provinces in front of the governors in accordance with the sacred constitutions of the deified brothers."[57] This seems to show the system of *coartación* at Rome. The slave appears to bargain with the owner for his freedom at a price. The slave pays the price "with his own money." The owner fails to perform his side of the bargain, and the slave is allowed to bring legal proceedings of an unusual kind against the owner. This is apparently a perfect representation of *coartación* at Rome. But things are not as they seem. Slaves at Rome had no property or money. As another text, *D.*40.1.4.1, explains, "bought with his own money" is a misnomer: it means paid for by money that did not come from the owner. Still, it is easy to see how *D.*40.1.5 *pr.* could have been an important link in establishing *coartación* in Spanish America. Indeed, *D*.40.1.4 *pr.* relates that the "deified brothers," Marcus Aurelius and Lucius Verus, had given a person "bought with his own cash" a status whereby he might secure freedom. *D*.40.1.5 *pr.* shows that what is involved is not regular court proceedings.

To return to the questions, it should first be noticed that *coartación* was not a creation of the state. It was not introduced by statute. Its origins are obscure, but it most plausibly arose when masters made such bargains with slaves, and on a failure to honor a bargain by an owner a slave brought suit (on analogy with the action of cruel treatment?) and the court allowed the action. Once this procedure became accepted, the next step would be to allow the slave an action to have a reasonable price fixed. Like the Roman approach, *coartación* benefited the owner: the slave would be more tractable and would work harder, and the owner would be able to buy a replacement. The fact that it gave legal security to the slave would not adversely affect any reasonable owner. The state was directly interested in *coartación* only insofar as it was taxable.

Coartación came into existence in a society where slavery was based on race. This is again explicable when we take account of how the system arose. It was not made from above by the government. Some owners made such bargains with some slaves. They would do so primarily because they thought it was to their advantage, and they could do so even if they were very racist. Even after *coartación* was fully established at law, it would not dramatically increase the freed population, especially not the black—as distinct from mulatto—freed population. It would be an exceptional slave who could earn for himself the amount he was valued at, even if the master observed the rule in the *Real Instrucción* of 31 May 1789, chapter 3, and allowed the slave to work for himself for two hours per day. One can readily imagine that very few agricultural workers—and the same chapter of the *Instrucción* states that slaves should be agricultural workers—would have the opportunity to earn so much. Most slaves would be unaware of the law. The few who could take advantage of *coartación* would tend to be urban slaves with a trade or particular skill, and most of these would be mulatto or quadroon or even less black.

It is appropriate at this stage to bring in a discussion of the categories of slaves who actually were manumitted. The evidence shows that proportionately more town slaves than country slaves were freed and that the majority of *inter vivos* manumissions were not gratuitous.[58] More females than males were freed.[59] This may well have been a consequence of an enduring sexual relationship between a slave woman and her owner. In this context, too, we should probably put the fact that prices for female slaves, especially of *ladinas* (those who had spent time in Spain before being sent to America) were higher than for males.[60] Children were frequently freed, and it would be unreasonable to believe that a fair proportion of them were not the owner's offspring. Others would owe their freedom to the affection shown to a child born in the household.[61] Domestic servants who had been loyal and were close to the owner are another important category.[62] Mulattoes were more commonly freed than blacks. Old and sick slaves, too weak to work, were at times rewarded with the treacherous gift of liberty,[63] an evil already dealt with in Roman legislation.[64] And it should be stressed that manumission by an owner was frequently regarded with suspicion or hostility by other free whites.[65] The bad character of blacks, whether slave or free, is emphasized again and again: their laziness, their thieving, their sexual license, and their violence.[66]

It was a feature of Spanish colonial law that local officials could suspend ordinances from Spain and had the right to suggest other rules in the light of their colonial experience.[67] The suspension was always regarded as temporary: if the king insisted on the law, new officials would be appointed to replace the old and to enforce the legislation. This dimension has to be borne in mind. When the *Real Cédula* of 31 May 1789 reached Caracas, Havana, Luisiana, Santo Domingo, and Tocaima (in Nueva Granada)—the very places where slaves were common—representations were made by petition about the very grave injuries that would follow its publication and its being put into effect. The problems are set out in an opinion of the Consejo de las Indias, dated 17 March 1794.[68] It was claimed that

at all times there were many crimes, murders, and insurrections arising from the insolence and insubordination of slaves to their masters
and majordomos. It was requested that in no way should the *Cédula*
be put into effect since with any attention at all the slaves became
arrogant and excited. It was argued that Spaniards treated their
slaves better than did the colonists of other lands, that if masters
committed some excess, they were branded as cruel, and all tribunals were open to the complaints of slaves. In fact, it was claimed,
Spanish gentleness to blacks was a cause of vituperation among foreigners. It was maintained that the *Cédula* was nothing but a repeti-
tion and amplification of existing Spanish laws, which were founded
on natural law, in the bonds of Christian charity and in the immutable rules of humanity; and, in addition, it corresponded to what
actually happened in practice. There was thus a stated support for
the provisions of the *Cédula,* except that because of the differences in
climate, customs, and persons in the colonies, there were difficulties
in applying the provisions literally.

The municipal councils of New Orleans and Santo Domingo
strengthened their representations with the examples ("which everyone cites") of thefts, murders, riots, and other crimes committed by
blacks, who were controlled only by a prudent rigor. It was also
claimed that if one took account of the disproportionate numbers of
blacks, their temperament and disposition, the distances between,
and situation of, the haciendas, one could not consider the fears of
insurrection unfounded. The distance between America and Spain,
the different climates, and the very different circumstances in America and Europe were stressed. The publication of the *Cédula,* it was
urged, would excite the blacks. What was in fact being requested
was not the revocation of the *Cédula* but the suspension of its effects,
and the tribunals and leaders, without publishing it, would act according to its spirit as cases arose. The king suspended resolution
until the war (with France) was finished.

The extent to which the petition is self-seeking, and nothing
more, is not easy to judge. In some of the Spanish possessions major
tasks allotted to slaves were unremitting and often dangerous, for
example, work in the sugar plantations and mines.[69] And examples

of extreme cruelty and savage oppression by owners abound.[70] One cannot fail to recognize in the low fertility rate of the female slaves at least some reflection of the hardships of their material life.[71] (It is surely not entirely without significance in this regard that, when the importation of slaves more or less stopped, only in continental English America did the slave population increase. Elsewhere it declined.)[72]

For slave law made in the colonies we can look at aspects of the *Código negro carolino* for Santo Domingo, issued at Santo Domingo in 1785, which has already been mentioned in connection with *coartación*.

The background to this code merits special attention. Its origins lie in the Royal Order of 23 December 1783 directed to the governor of Santo Domingo from the minister for the Indies, ordering the formation of rules for the economic, political, and moral governing of the blacks of the island to conform to those in the French *Code noir*.[73] The Spanish part of the island had been in economic decline for more than a century, in sharp contrast to the prosperity of the French part. The reason was seen to reside in the large slave population in the French part, which permitted intensive cultivation, and the strict control of slaves.[74] Important local citizens, "as being informed on the matter," were consulted, and their views both of what was wrong in the Spanish part and of what had to be done largely coincided. The task of drafting the code was given to D. Agustín Emparán y Orbe, and he presented the draft on 14 December 1784.[75] The legal sources that influenced the code included, as well as the French *Code noir,* Spanish legislation and Roman law. The attorney general much praised the draft, and, after some delay and minor changes (including the name), it received the formal approval of the Real Audiencia on 16 March 1785 and was transmitted to Spain. The difficulties that then ensued for its promulgation by the king—including the death of Carlos III and the appearance of the *Real Cédula* of 1789—need not concern us. What counts is that, in contrast to the legislation emanating from Spain, this *Código,* which was far more severe toward slaves, was the result of attitudes on the spot.

The proemium recounts the decline of Hispaniola over two centuries and gives among the reasons the small number of blacks and slaves, their laziness, their independent spirit, arrogance, thefts, and other abuses. Progress would be accelerated if the island were populated with black cultivators. Law should deal with the useful occupation of free blacks and slaves in cultivation, the division of them into classes and races, the tasks in which they should be employed, their complete subordination to officials, to their masters, and to white people, and with rewards for good service and penal laws for their correction. All this should be cemented on the principles of good education and complete instruction in the Catholic religion.

The first chapter pronounces in law 4 that religion is the first object and ornament of good government. It should serve this purpose all the more for slaves and blacks, whose wretched situation was rewarded with the true light they would acquire by their translation to the lands of His Majesty. Religious observance is then imposed. Chapter 2 says blacks should not be considered solely as automata useful for the painful tasks of agriculture; it further states that slaves are superstitious and easily given to insurrection and vengeance and are naturally inclined to poisoning. Hence these inclinations must be restrained, and there should be substituted feelings of loyalty to the sovereign, love of the Spanish nation, gratitude to their masters, subordination to the whites, respect for their elders, and so on.

Chapter 3, laws 1 and 2, divide the colored population into classes or races such as *pardo* (mulatto), *tercerones, cuarterones,* and so on. Law 5 enacts that every black, slave or free, *primerizo* or *tercerón* and on up will be as submissive and respectful to every white person, as if each one of them was his owner or master. Law 6 closes public schools to all blacks and mulattoes because they are destined to work in agriculture and must not mix with whites, *tercerones,* and so on. Under law 7 a black or mulatto who fails in some way to respect a white is to be placed in the pillory or iron ring in the square and be given twenty-five lashes; if the defaulter is a *tercerón, cuarterón,* or *mestizo,* he will suffer four days of imprisonment and a fine of twenty-five pesos. Law 8 punishes a black or mulatto who raises his hand, stick, or stone against any white with one hundred lashes, two years of imprisonment on short rations and with no pay, with fetters on his foot, and for the same offense imposes a smaller penalty on other persons of mixed race who have more white blood. Under law 10, a slave who raises his hand, stick, or stone against his master, causing bruising or bleeding, or gives the master's children or wife a slap will, without fail, be put to death. Law 11 lays down that no black, mulatto, *cuarterón*, or *mestizo* may reproach or contradict white people, except in very submissive terms, even if he knows he is right, or raise his voice elatedly or arrogantly, or complain to his superiors of any injury they have done him, and penalties are provided.

Chapter 9 contains sumptuary laws. For instance, law 2 decrees that no blacks, free or slave, or mulattoes may use mantillas (which were usually of silk or lace) in place of *paños* (head coverings of coarser stuff), nor may blacks wear at the waist a sword or staff, or a sombrero braided with gold or silver (unless they are officials of some organized militia), and neither one nor the other may wear garments of silk.

Chapter 17, law 1, decrees that slaves have no legal personality and cannot acquire the slightest right of possession or ownership which is not for the benefit of the owner. Law 2 makes the owner liable for contracts of slaves he has set up in business, and law 4 puts slaves in the category of other animate beings. Chapter 18 regulates the slaves' *peculium*, which is given full recognition. I have already discussed manumission and the severe restrictions on it. Slaves, according to chapter 23, law 1, can be criminal defendants but otherwise cannot be parties to a criminal or civil action.

The background to this slave code must be stressed. Santo Domingo had few slaves or free blacks but wanted many more for the economic development of the island. But the blacks were wanted under "good" legal rules.

The *Código negro carolino* and the arguments reported in the opinion of the Consejo de las Indias dated 17 March 1794 leave little doubt that if the law in Spanish America for the treatment of slaves had been made on the spot it would have become openly racist, there would have been severe restrictions on the manumission of slaves, and free blacks of whatever degree would have been, at law, much worse off than whites.[76] It was Roman law, its Reception in Spain, the accession of the Spanish colonies to the kingdom of Castile, and thus the transplanting of Castilian slave law to the New World that made manumission easy in the Spanish colonies. Governments' habitual lack of interest in legislation for private law and the force of the legal tradition kept the Roman structure largely intact.

Local regulations were frequently made in the colonies restricting the employment of blacks or mulattoes. These affected above all gold- and silver-working—at some times and places only Spaniards might become craft masters—but they might also relate to carpenters or polishers.[77] Spanish colonies also occasionally imposed such restrictions as forbidding painters or gilders to have apprentices who were not Spanish.[78] Most restrictions concerned who could become notaries,[79] though a *Real Cédula* of 14 February 1717 addressed to the archbiship of Los Reyes prohibits the grant of the office of *caniculario* (beadle, who chases dogs out of churches) to blacks or mulattoes; the office may be held only by Spanish subjects.[80] Likewise, bastards could not be notaries. The restriction here is to be read in the light of the restrictions placed on university education, once universities were founded. In general, these were closed to blacks, mulattoes, and all categories of slaves,[81] and even to quadroons.[82] These laws, except when (as happened) exceptions were made, would exclude such persons from the higher professions such as medicine.

As we shall see, these restrictions on slaves and free blacks being educated or working in certain areas were minor compared with the situation in English America.[83]

4

ENGLAND AND SLAVE LAW
IN AMERICA

The legal situation of the English colonies and of the slaveholding states in the United States that developed from them was to prove very different from that in Latin American countries. There was no slavery in England, hence there was no slave law in England.[1] And there had been no Reception of Roman law. Certainly, Roman law was at times made use of in England, but there was no tradition of relying on it for legal development. Thus Roman slave law in whole or in large measure could not be automatically taken over for the English colonies. A law of slavery had to be made from scratch.

The failure to receive Roman law in England entailed a further fundamental difference between the Spanish and Portuguese colonies and the English colonies. As we have seen, medieval civilian learning adopted for public law the Roman private law doctrine of *accessio* and applied it to the acquisition of territory so that when lands of infidels were acquired by a Christian prince, these territories were incorporated into the prince's land. Hence the law of the home state was automatically the law of the colony. But with no Reception of Roman law in England there was no acceptance of this notion of *accessio,* which was foreign to English law. William Blackstone divides colonies into two species: those that were previously uninhabited and those that were conquered or ceded.[2] In the latter, the existing laws continue unless and until the king changes them, provided they are not against the law of God. Blackstone goes on to state:

Our American plantations are principally of this latter sort, being obtained in the last century either by right of conquest and driving out the natives (with what natural justice I shall not at present enquire) or by treaties. And therefore the common law of England, as such, has no allowance or authority there; they being no part of the mother country, but distinct (though dependent) dominions. They are subject however to the control of the parliament; though (like Ireland, Man, and the rest) not bound by any acts of parliament, unless particularly named. The form of government in most of them is borrowed from that of England. They have a governor named by the king, (or in some proprietary colonies by the proprietor) who is his representative or deputy. They have courts of justice of their own, from whose decisions an appeal lies to the king in council here in England. Their general assemblies which are their house of commons, together with their council of state being their upper house, with the concurrence of the king or his representative the governor, make laws suited to their own emergencies. But it is particularly declared by statute 7 & 8 W. III.c.22. That all laws, by-laws, usages, and customs, which shall be in practice in any of the plantations, repugnant to any law, made or to be made in this kingdom relative to the said plantations, shall be utterly void and of no effect.

The difference in Spanish and English law here is fundamental. The law of the Spanish colonies was the law of Castile as it was and as it would become.[3] Law could only be made in the colonies by governors, viceroys, or others to the extent that power to do so had been expressly granted by the ruler of Castile. The lawmaking power remained in Spain. In the English colonies, the basic laws were those made by the colonists in the colonies.[4]

Slavery as a social institution was accepted in the English colonies without legal authorization.[5] Thus, in the early days in the colonies overall, there were slaves but no law of slavery. The law came into being bit by bit, either by statute or by judicial precedent, sometimes based on what people did.[6] The statutes on slavery, as on other matters, were not made in England but in the local legislatures. Thus they were more geared to local conditions than was the law in Spanish or Portuguese colonies. Judges were faced with the task of creating the law when there was no statute in point, and it became a common practice, especially from the late eighteenth century onward,[7] as exemplified in the Virginia case of *Commonwealth*

v. *Turner* (discussed in the first chapter), to turn for guidance to Roman law, often through the medium of Thomas Cooper's edition of the *Institutes* of Justinian[8] or of John Taylor, *Elements of the Civil Law,* first published in 1755. The words of Luther Cushing, quoted in the first chapter, that in the absence of legislation the authority of Roman law was recognized and applied, are not without validity. Thus for South Carolina, for example, between 1812 and 1859 several reported cases expressly referred to Roman law.[9] Its significance is underlined even when its authority is rejected as by Harper, J. in *Tidyman* v. *Rose,* Rich. Eq. Cas. 294, in 1832: "But still it [civil law] is not our law; the Court has no legislative power; and where the common law is not doubtful, we have no right to supersede it by provisions, which may appear to us better and more reasonable." Yet Harper praises its merit and its usefulness when the common law is doubtful.[10] More to the point, he goes on to say of the rule that he wishes to reject: "But indeed I do not perceive that the rule referred to, is the doctrine of the civil law." And he spends considerable effort showing that it is not the doctrine of the civil law. It was also standard, but not universal, practice for judges to observe that villenage in England was not slavery and did not provide a useful analogy for developing slave law.[11]

I stress this use of Roman law not just because it played a role in the development of the law but because the use itself can be explained only in terms of judicial culture. Those making the law in whatever capacity, whether as legislators or as subordinate, restricted judges or jurists, shape the law in part through their own tradition.

But judges did not have the power to make sweeping innovations—that power was reserved to the legislature. So the law of slavery in general was largely statute law. The general picture is well known. Throughout the eighteenth century legislatures passed numerous statutes imposing ever greater restrictions on slaves and free blacks.

But the imposing bulk of legislation on slavery and free blacks should not lead to the conclusion that the general thesis set out in the first chapter, that governments are not usually much interested in private law, is mistaken. There are two aspects to the issue. The first is that slavery in English America was a special case. The law in general was well developed, but slavery was a social institution, new to the legal system and completely unregulated by law. More law was needed faster than it could be supplied by subordinates in the system such as judges. The legislature had to become involved. The second is that much of the legislation concerns public rather than private law.[12]

English slave law possesses a public dimension in a way that is in sharp contrast with Roman law. Apart from "traditional" criminal law, the state and the other citizens at Rome were not much involved with the slave and the owner. For example, no one could interfere with a slave except at the master's instigation. If the slave ran away, his capture was the master's business. No citizen group was organized to find the runaway. On recapture, it was the master's business to decide whether and how severely the slave was to be punished. It was up to the master to decide what clothing the slave wore, how he was to be educated, the training he was to receive, and the work he was to do. The slave could make contracts with the master's permission, could live wherever the master wished, could indulge in whatever activities (which were otherwise lawful) that the master allowed. In contrast, in English America one might almost say that a slave belonged to every citizen—at least he was subordinate to every white. Thus a slave off a plantation could be stopped by any white and questioned on his activities. Citizens were organized by law in patrols to recapture runaways. Penalties were laid down for each offense of running away; if within a certain time the master did not inflict them the state would. The government declared that only appropriate clothing was to be worn, and it might even determine what clothing was appropriate. The state intervened in the education of slaves even to the extent of prohibiting teaching them to read or write. Slaves could not buy and sell as their master wished, they could not live apart from the master whenever he wished, they could not keep horses, cattle, and pigs; they could not, even if the master would allow it, hire out their time. These rules did not apply at all times and in all colonies or states, but they do give the flavor of the general law.

For our purposes it is enough to look at one state, South Carolina.[13] No two states were alike, and none can be declared typical. But the law of one is enough for illustration.

South Carolina was atypical in two ways. First, it was the only colony or state that was settled from the beginning by slaveholders. Slavery did not develop there as it did, for instance, in Maryland, Delaware, or Pennsylvania, but was there from the start under the control of colonists who had experience with slavery in Barbados. Second, South Carolina was the only state, apart from Mississippi in the 1850s, that had a black majority.[14] But these features only emphasize that the law was not so very different from elsewhere in English America.

In what follows little will be said about changes in political and economic conditions in South Carolina. I am well aware that the South Carolina of 1700 was a very different place from the South Carolina of 1850. South Carolina had been a colony of England and had become a state of the United States. Its economy had been transformed by the successful introduction of rice.[15] Naturally, these changes had an impact on the law. But the relation of the rules of slave law to conditions in society has been well explained by others. Here I wish simply to note the role of borrowing in the growth of the law and to emphasize that there was a pattern of development. Social, economic, political, and religious conditions in Rome, too, changed dramatically. But little need be said of these changes in tracing the development of Roman slave law from the city-state in the Italian peninsula in the fifth century B.C. to the Byzantine Empire centered on Constantinople in the sixth century A.D. My purpose in this chapter is to point out the contrast between the slave law of English America on one hand and of Rome and the rest of America on the other.

Settlement began in South Carolina in 1669, by which time slavery was already well established in the English West Indies and was growing in Virginia. The colony was settled from Barbados and other of the islands, and the settlers brought their slaves with them. Slavery was envisaged from the start, as the 110th section of *The Fundamental Constitutions of Carolina* (1669) shows: "Every free man of Carolina, shall have absolute power and authority over his negro slaves, of what opinion or religion soever."[16] This is the sole relevant provision of the *Fundamental Constitutions,* and it takes for granted the existence of slaves and the institution of slavery. Moreover, only black slaves are envisaged. The punctuation of the provision with a comma after "Carolina" links the preceding phrase with the last part of the sentence. That is, the import of the provision is that whatever religion is professed by a free man, his slaves are in his absolute power and authority. The provision has to be read then with section 109: "No person whatsoever shall disturb, molest, or persecute another, for his speculative opinions in religion, or his way of worship."[17] The philosopher John Locke was probably at least partially the author of the *Fundamental Constitutions.*[18] It is not certain that they ever passed into law. It is ironic that the main point of the provision, which incidentally reveals that slavery is envisaged, concerns freedom of religion.

The first South Carolina statute specifically on slavery is the Act for the Better Ordering of Slaves of as early as 1690. It derives in great measure from a statute of Barbados of two years earlier, an Act for the governing of Negroes of 1688.[19] The dependence is evident in clause 5 of the Barbados statute:

> And be it further enacted and ordained, that if any Negro or Slave whatsoever, shall offer any violence to any Christian, by striking or the like, such Negro or other Slave, shall for his or her first offense, by Information given upon oath to the next Justice, be severely whipped by the Constable, by order of the said Justice; for his second offense of that nature, by order of the Justice of the Peace, he shall be severely whipped, his nose slit, and be burned in some part of his face with a hot iron: And for his third offense, he shall receive by order of the Governor and Council, such greater punishment as they shall think meet to inflict.

Part of the first section of the South Carolina statute reads:

> And if any negro or Indian slave shall offer any violence, by striking or the like, to any white person, he shall for the first offense be severely whipped by the constable, by order of any justice of peace; and for the second offense, by like order, shall be severely whipped, his or her nose

slit, and face burnt in some place; and for the third offense, to be left to two justices and three sufficient freeholders, to inflict death, or any other punishment, according to their discretion; Provided, such striking or conflict be not by command of or in lawful defense of their owner's persons.

Borrowing is the nature of the legal game. Indeed, the law of South Carolina was to serve as the model for the law of some other states. Most notably, Georgia's slave code of 1755, which is entitled An Act for the Better Ordering and Governing of Negroes and Other Slaves in this Province, is directly derived from South Carolina's act of 1740, which bears exactly the same title.

The contrast between the law of South Carolina and that of Rome should be noticed. In Roman law violence by a slave against a free person was not mentioned as a specific offense. At the most, the lowly status of the offender would increase the insult to the victim, who might thereby obtain greater damages from the owner if he sued on the *actio iniuriarum* of private law. The 1690 act, also in the first section, provides:

> That no person whatsoever shall send or give leave to any negro or Indian slave, under his or their care, charge or ownership, to go out of their plantations, unless such as usually wait on their persons, without a ticket, or one or more white men in their company, in which ticket shall be expressed their names and numbers, and also, from and to what place they are intended for, and time, on penalty of forty shillings, and paying for taking up such slave as a runaway.[20]

The same section provides that anyone who does not attempt to apprehend any slave without a ticket who comes on to his plantation and, having apprehended the slave, does not punish him with a moderate whipping is to be fined.

Section 19 of the Act for the Better Ordering and Governing of Negroes and Slaves of 1712 makes running away a criminal offense and imposes obligations on owners. A slave over age sixteen who runs away and stays away for twenty days is, for a first offense, to be publicly and severely whipped, not exceeding forty lashes, at the procurement of the owner or his overseer. If the owner fails to administer such punishment within ten days, anyone may complain within one month to a justice of the peace, who will order the slave to be whipped at the master's expense. For a second offense the master is obliged under threat of a fine of ten pounds to brand R on the slave's right cheek; for a third offense, under threat of a fine of twenty pounds, to whip severely and cut off one of the slave's ears; for a fourth offense, under threat of losing property in the slave to the complainant, to castrate a male slave and brand R on the left cheek of a female slave. The section provides that if a slave should die as a consequence of castration, without neglect on the part of whoever ordered it, the owner will be compensated from the public treasury. For a fifth offense the slave is to be tried before two justices of the peace, who may "order the cord of one of the slave's legs to be cut off above the heel, or else to pronounce sentence of death upon the slave."

Section 28 of the same act forbade masters, under penalty of a fine, to allow their slaves to go and work wherever the slaves pleased on condition that the slaves give the masters a determined sum of money.[21] An additional act to an act entitled An Act for the better Ordering and Governing Negroes and all other Slaves of 1714 provided in section 11:

> And be it further enacted by the authority aforesaid, That no person whatsoever, after the first day of March next, shall suffer or allow any of his or their slaves to plant for themselves any corn, peas or rice, or to keep for themselves any stock of hogs, cattle or horses, under the penalty of twenty pounds current money of this Province, for every slave so suffered or allowed to plant any corn, peas or rice, or to keep any of such stock, as aforesaid; the penalty to be covered by bill, plaint or information, in any court of record in this Province, the one half to be paid to him or them who will inform and sue for the same, and the other half to the public receiver, for the use of the public.

An act of 1722 declares in section 35: "And whereas, great inconveniences do arise from negroes and other slaves keeping and breeding of horses, whereby they convey intelligences from one part of the country to another, and carry on their secret plots and contrivances for insurrections and rebellions." Illogically perhaps in view of this reason, the section bars slaves from keeping not only horses but also cattle and hogs.[22]

By section 19 of an act of 1735 owners were compelled to pay twenty shillings plus twelve pence per mile for mileage to anyone who brought back a runaway slave. Section 36 of the same act declared, "And whereas, many of the slaves in this Province wear clothes much above the condition of slaves, for the procuring whereof they use sinister and evil methods" and hence the wearing of clothes (other than livery) "finer, other or of greater value" than defined categories such as duffelds and scotch plaids was prohibited.[23] Although sumptuary legislation existed in Rome,[24] none of it mentioned extravagance by slaves.

Section 45 of the 1740 act forbade teaching writing to slaves, and this prohibition was extended to teaching reading by an Act to Amend the Laws in Relation to Slaves and Free Persons of Color of 1834, section 1. An Additional and Explanatory Act to an Act of the General Assembly of this Province, entitled An Act for the better Ordering and Governing Negroes and other Slaves in this Province, and for continuing such part of the said act as was not altered or amended by this present act, for the term therein mentioned of 1751 forbade in section 11 physicians, apothecaries, and druggists to employ slaves where they kept medicines or drugs, and in section 12 stated that no slave was to administer medicine to any other slave except by the direction of a white. These provisions were in response to a fear of poisoning.[25]

An Act respecting Slaves, Free Negroes, Mulattoes and Mestizoes; for enforcing the more punctual performance of Patroll Duty; and to impose certain restrictions on the emancipation of Slaves of 1800, section 1, declared the assemblies even of free blacks to be illegal if they were in a confined space to which free entrance was prevented.

More examples could be adduced, but enough has been said to illustrate that, much more than in Rome, slavery in South Carolina was seen as a relationship not just between the slave and the owner but also between slaves and their owners on the one hand and the society at large on the other. Slave law had a public dimension, which shows that apparently slavery in ancient Rome was a very different social institution from slavery in English America.[26] This public dimension to slave law in English America appears very clearly from the digested statutes of other states such as that of Alabama of 1843 and of the 1855 Revised Code of North Carolina, chapter 107: Slaves and Free Negroes.

The government's lack of interest in private law aspects of slavery is as striking as its involvement in the life of the slaves. Thus nothing is said in the statutes about slave marriages, though they were not recognized as having legal validity.[27] Nothing is said about the validity or otherwise of appointing by will slaves as heirs or legatees, whether the testator was the owner or another. No statutory provision regulates the acquisition of ownership or possession through a slave when more than one person has real rights, such as a liferent, over him or her. There are no provisions regulating something akin to the Roman *peculium,* though, in view of the prohibitions on slaves keeping horses, cattle, and pigs for their own use, it was understood that owners did allow slaves to have control over some possessions.

Slaves had no legal personality and were firmly classed as things. As early as section 2 of the 1690 act, slaves are described as chattels. But as the provisions already mentioned show, they were a unique kind of property, and they were treated in law in a unique way. Since they lacked legal personality, slaves could be neither plaintiffs nor defendants in civil actions, nor could they be active in bringing a criminal suit. But they could, of course, be defendants in criminal actions. Indeed, though we need not elaborate, there was, in contrast to Rome, a separate criminal legal system for slaves. Procedure for slaves' crimes was more summary, penalties were more severe when the offender was a slave, and there were crimes that in effect could only be committed by slaves.[28] Some aspects of this criminal law system have been noticed in passing. Part of section 1 of the first law on slaves, of 1690, has already been quoted. It provided punishment for any slave who struck any white person.[29] A few other details will be sufficient. Section 17 of the act of 1735 even extended the effect of the provisions to blows struck by a free black. In section

8 of the 1690 act there is the presumably economically efficient but arbitrary proviso:

> *Provided nevertheless,* that when and as often as any of the aforementioned crimes be committed by more than one negro that shall deserve death, that then and in all such cases, only one of the said criminals shall suffer death, as exemplary, the rest to be returned to the owners, which owners of slaves so offending, shall bear proportionably the loss of the said negro so put to death, and also proportionably the damage done by the said criminals to the party or parties injured, as shall be allotted them by the said justices and freeholders; and if any person shall refuse to pay his part so allotted him, that then and in all such cases, the said justices and freeholders are hereby required to issue out their warrant of distress upon the goods and chattels of the person so refusing, and shall cause the same to be sold by the public outcry, to satisfy the said money so allowed him to pay, and to return the overplus, if any be, to the owner.[30]

A corollary appears in later legislation:

> And *whereas,* it has been found by experience, that the executing of several negroes for felonies of a smaller nature, by which they have been condemned to die, have been of great charge and expense to the public, and will continue (if some remedy be not found,) to be very chargeable and burthensome to this Province; *Be it therefore enacted* by the authority aforesaid, That all negroes or other slaves who shall be convicted and found guilty of any capital crime, (murder excepted,) for which they used to receive sentence of death, as the law directs, shall be transported from this Province, by the public receiver for the time being, to any other of his Majesty's plantations, or other foreign part, where he shall think fitting to send them for the use of the public; and the said slave or slaves shall be appraised as the law directs, by the justices and freeholders, or a quorum of them, and the value of the said slave or slaves so appraised shall be paid to the master or owner thereof, out of the public treasury, and the public receiver for the time being is hereby empowered and required to pay the same.[31]

In several regards for criminal law free blacks were treated in the same way as slaves.[32]

Slave testimony was not usually admissible but might be allowed in certain instances of crimes when the defendant was a slave or a free black. Thus, by article 13 of the act of 1712, the evidence of one slave might be sufficient for conviction of another in all petty larcenies or trespasses not exceeding forty shillings. But no free black or slave was to suffer loss of limb or life, except on confession, or by the oath of Christian evidence, or the positive evidence of two slaves. Article 14 of the act of 1735 made the evidence of one slave sufficient against another charged with making or conspiring to make an insurrection or mutiny or to arise against the white people or with any other capital crime. The act of 1720, section 13, allowed the evidence of one slave without oath to be sufficient against another slave charged with any crime or offense. Directly in one situation and indirectly in another by the 1722 act slave testimony might be good against a white. Section 4 provides that if a slave entrusted with a gun or cutlass shot or killed another person's cattle, sheep, or hogs, or lent the gun or cutlass to someone who did likewise, the slave's owner shall pay to the injured party double the value of the cattle, hogs, or sheep, and that the evidence of two slaves may be sufficient. The principal offender is the slave. Section 12 enacted that for the first two times that a slave broke open corn-houses or rice-houses under pretense of hunger he would not suffer death but lesser penalties, and the master would have to make good the full amount of the loss. Testimony of two slaves was sufficient.

The laws allowed scope for cruelty to a slave, both by the owner and others. Thus section 12 of the 1690 act states:

> And it is further enacted by the authority aforesaid, That if any slave, by punishment from the owner for running away or other offense, shall suffer in life or limb, no person shall be liable to the law for the same; but if any one out of wilfulness, wantoness, or bloody mindedness, shall kill a slave, he or she, upon due conviction thereof, shall suffer three months imprisonment, without bail or mainprize, and also pay the sum of fifty pounds to the owner of such slave.

The act of 1712, section 30, declared that a person who wantonly killed his own slave would pay fifty pounds into the public treasury; one who wantonly killed another's slave would pay the owner the full value and twenty-five pounds into the public treasury but would suffer no other penalty. The 1722 act, section 31, increased the penalty for wantonly killing another's slave to fifty pounds. The 1735 act, section 28, increased the penalties for wantonly killing one's own or another's slave to five hundred pounds. If he could not pay, he was to be whipped, not exceeding thirty-nine lashes, and serve the slave's owner for three years. The act of 1720, section 6, established penalties for improperly beating another's slave.

The manumission of slaves was at first unregulated by statute, and section 1 of the 1712 act simply assumes that slaves could be freed by their masters or, for good cause, by the governor or provincial council. A similar assumption recurs in section 1 of the act of 1735, but section 35 provides that a master manumitting a slave "for any particular merit or service" must make provision for the slave to leave the province. If the slave did not leave the province within six months, he would be reenslaved and sold by the public treasurer. Section 7 of the act of 1800, after relating that it had been a practice to free slaves of bad character or who were incapable of gaining an honest livelihood, declares that an owner who wished to manumit must inform some justice, who would summon five freeholders to meet. They would examine the owner under oath and if satisfied that the slave was not of bad character and was capable of earning a living they would issue a certificate to that effect. Under section 8 no manumission would be valid unless it was by deed recorded in the court of the district and was accompanied by the certificate of fitness. The Act to restrain the emancipation of slaves, and to prevent Free persons of Color from entering into this State; and for other purposes, of 1820, section 1, declared that no slaves could be freed except by an act of the legislature. Various statutes which need not be enumerated controlled and prohibited the entry into the state of slaves or free blacks. An act of 1822, section 1, enacted that free blacks—who must have been the descendants of slaves freed before 1735—who left the state would not be permitted to return. Finally, on manumission the act of 1690, section 2, states that becoming a Christian did not make a slave free.[33]

There can be no doubt that the intense interest of the South Carolina legislature in slavery, the public dimension of slave law, the overall thrust of the legislation, and the discriminatory treatment of freedmen and free blacks were all the products of racism.[34] Indeed, racism obviously accounts for the sharp contrast between the ancient Roman slave law and that in English America. Since it was only in English America that a slave law grew up *de novo* with slavery based on race, that law ought to be the paradigm case for racist slavery. And Roman law is the paradigm case for nonracist slavery. It is this difference which makes particularly instructive the South Carolina cases concerning emancipation or attempted emancipation and related issues after statutes were passed restricting emancipation. Case law is important for this topic.

In *Bynum* v. *Walker* of 1812, a bequest of slaves with directions to set them free according to law was held to be an attempt to evade the statute of 1800, which expressly forbade emancipation except by deed executed in the lifetime of the master, a certain time before his death, in a prescribed form.

In 1822 Martin Staggers executed a will leaving five female slaves with their future issue to his brother, then after his death they were to be free to all intents and purposes forever. There was also a legacy to the brother with the remainder to the slaves. In the resulting lawsuit, *Blakely* v. *Tisdale*,[35] though the legal point no longer had to be decided (in 1868), it was claimed, "But it is plausible to suggest that Martin Staggers' will affords an early instance of an attempt, such as afterwards became frequent, to evade the act of 1820, by conferring substantial freedom under nominal slavery, and thus the gift to the slaves may be relieved from the effect of precedent contingency."

A clause of Ann McCants's will read: "To my friends and executors . . . I leave my wench, Nancy, and her children, Louisa and Mary, and her future issue, by reason of her faithful services, and my wench, Mary Horry, a mulatto, and her child, Augustus, and any other children she may have, with this special charge, that no other service or wages shall be required of them than may be sufficient to pay their taxes." Legacies were also left to the slaves. The decision of the chancellor on circuit was that this was contrary to the subsequent act of 1841, which provided "that any bequest, gift or conveyance, of any slave or slaves, accompanied with a trust or confidence, either secret or expressed, that such slave or slaves shall be held in nominal servitude only, shall be void and of no effect; and every donee or trustee holding under such bequest, gift or conveyance, shall be liable to deliver up such slave, or held to account for the value, for the benefit of the distributees or next of kin of the person making such bequest, gift or conveyance." Chancellor Caldwell held to the contrary in the Court of Errors and declared:

> 1. That the pecuniary gifts to the said slaves, and other provisions directed for their comfort, violate no law whatever, not even the Act of 1841, but are as consistent with the laws of South Carolina as they are with the dictates of humanity. 2. That the directions contained in the will, relative to the time and services of the said slaves, are conditions of the bequest to the defendants, and not trusts, and being conditions subsequent do not invalidate the gift. 3. That even if these directions be regarded as trusts, they were not illegal at the death of the testatrix, and cannot be rendered so by the subsequent enactment of the Act of 1841.[36]

Another similar case is *Skrine* v. *Walker*[37] of 1851. In *Vose* v. *Hannahan*[38] of 1857 there was a deed of gift, executed a few days before the owner's death, of his slaves with a secret trust that the slaves should be held in nominal servitude only. The administrator of the deceased's estate claimed that the deed was void by section 3 of the 1841 act, which has just been quoted. Judge John Belton O'Neall held that a secret trust would not make the gift void against the donor and that an administrator could not dispute the gift of his intestate. The deed, he held, is void only "for the benefit of the distributees or next of kin of the donor," and thus they alone could bring an action for its rescission.

Slaveowners might even, for reasons of conscience, desire to emancipate all their slaves. Thus John Clarkson wrote on 7 October 1840, for the attention of his executor:

> To William Clarkson.—By my will all my property will come into your hands on certain conditions, or on your declining to take it, into the possession of the Rev. William H. Barnwell, on the same condi-

tions. Some of these conditions I now express in writing. All of my negroes must be emancipated, either immediately or at any time the Rev. Wm. H. Barnwell shall think advisable. Should immediate emancipation be deemed inexpedient, the proceeds arising from the lands and negroes, must be placed at interest until they are liberated, and then this accumulated sum, together with the sale of my lands and other moneys not specifically appropriated, shall be given to them, that is, my land and all the proceeds shall be considered their property. If the law forbidding the emancipation of slaves in South Carolina is then in force, so that all my negroes must be removed, then the husbands or wives of any of mine belonging to other persons, must be purchased from monies of my estate not vested in lands, if there is a sufficient amount, but if there is not a sufficient sum, then so much as is necessary in addition, must be taken from the sale of the lands. The purchase is only to be made, provided no arrangement can be effected by which the husband and wives will not be separated. If there is any amount left after the purchase of the negroes and without using the funds arising from the sale of the lands, then two hundred dollars is to be given to the Ladies' Benevolent Society of Charleston, and the remainder to the Domestic and Foreign Missionary Society of the United States of America, provided there is as much as six hundred dollars left. But if there is not so much, then the Domestic and Foreign Missionary Society is to receive twice as much as the Ladies' Benevolent Society of whatever sum is left; but should there be more, the Ladies' Benevolent Society is only to receive the two hundred dollars, and the domestic and Foreign Missionary Society the remainder, whatever it may be. I wish (if possible) that the negroes should not be sent out of America. I will expect you or the Rev. Mr. Barnwell, whoever receives the property, to make a will providing for the emancipation of my negroes, together with their husbands and wives belonging to other persons as stated above, if the negroes must be sent and remain out of the neighborhood. The Rev. W. H. Barnwell must be advised with in every case that I do not determine in writing or orally. Whatever oral directions I may give are to be considered my will in preference to this, although verbal.

And on 25 November 1842 he wrote again: "Husbands and wives must on no account be separated." The testator's intentions failed because of the provisions of the act of 1841 and also because these papers, being executed after the will and not attested by three witnesses, could not be admitted in evidence as testamentary papers.[39]

There are many other cases which seem to show attempts, successful or failed, to emancipate slaves despite the restrictions.[40] Four deserve special mention.

In 1830 John Carmille by deed assigned

> the said negroes, Henrietta, Charlotte, Francis, Nancy, and John, on the special trust, confidence and condition, that they will, from time to time, and at all times, hereafter, permit and suffer the negroes above named, or any or all of them, and also the future issue and increase of the females, to seek out and procure employment, and to work out for their own maintenance and support; and further, in trust, to allow them, the said negroes, &c., to receive and take, for their sole use and benefit, all such moneys as they might obtain for their labor, or otherwise, after paying to the trustees the sum of one dollar per annum, and no more.

In the ensuing case of *Carmille* v. *Carmille's Administrator*,[41] O'Neall, J. was able to hold that the deed (and another which we may ignore) was valid and that it vested title to the slaves in the grantees; that if the grantees gave the slaves the fruits of their labor that was not unlawful; and that slaves might hold and acquire personal property with the owner's consent, and the property was the owner's. It was stated in court that Henrietta had been Carmille's mistress and that the other slaves were their children.[42]

A second case is *Willis* v. *Jollitte*.[43] In 1852 Elijah Willis executed a will in which he directed his executors to take his slave Amy and her seven children to Ohio and there emancipate them. He bequeathed the rest of his estate, real and personal, to his executors in trust for Amy and the children. In 1855 he went to Ohio with Amy and the children to emancipate them, but he died a few minutes after landing in Cincinnati. It was held that this act of taking the slaves to Ohio to free them was sufficient for emancipation, and therefore the trusts in their favor in the will were valid. It was made clear in the evidence that Amy was Willis's mistress and that he was the father of some of her children.

The third case, *Thorne* v. *Fordham* 4 Rich. Eq. 222, which was heard in 1852, related, however, to a will that had come into effect in 1824, the day after it was made. A clause of the will provided: "All the rest of all my real and personal estate I give unto Richard Fordham, to be held in trust by him for John, Thomas, Philip, Rebecca, Caroline, and Susan Thorne, persons of color, and their heirs forever, to be applied to the sole use and benefit of them, the said John, Thomas, Philip, Rebecca, Caroline and Susan." The trust was treated as valid. John, Thomas, Philip, Caroline, and Susan were recognized by the testator as his natural children by Rebecca Thorne, a former slave of his and whom he had emancipated in 1811. The issue before the court was whether the Rebecca named in the will was this Rebecca Thorne or another Rebecca born a slave to a mother called Judy, and whom the testator and also his executor claimed to be their natural daughter.[44]

These cases were occurring against a background of extreme racism, which judges shared. Thus in *Gordon* v. *Blackman* 1 Rich. Eq. 61 in 1844, another attempted emancipation case, the chancellor declared:

> This is another of those cases, multiplying of late with a fearful rapidity, in which the superstitious weakness of dying men, proceeding from an astonishing ignorance of the solid moral and scriptural foundations upon which the institution of slavery rests, and from a total inattention to the shock which their conduct is calculated to give to the whole frame of our social policy, induces them, in their last moments, to emancipate their slaves, in fraud of the indubitable and declared policy of the State.

And in another, similar case in 1854, *Morton* v. *Thompson* 6 Rich. Eq. 370, Dargan, Ch. said:

> A free African population is a curse to any country, slaveholding or non-slaveholding; and the evil is exactly proportionated to the number of such population. This race, however conducive they may be in a state of slavery, to the advance of civilization, (by the results of their valuable labors,) in a state of freedom, and in the midst of a civilized community, are a dead weight to the progress of improvement. With

few exceptions they become drones and lazaroni—consumers, without being producers. Uninfluenced by the higher incentives of human action, and governed mainly by the instincts of animal nature, they make no provision for the morrow, and look only to the wants of the passing hour. As an inevitable result, they become pilferers and marauders, and corrupters of the slaves. Our early colonial legislation bears the impress of these great truths in the repeated enactments discouraging and restricting the emancipation of slaves. In this state of the law, there were not wanting attempts at evasions. Some of these attempts were successful. I am constrained to say, (and I say it with all proper deference,) that, in my opinion, the Judiciary did not seem to realize the stern, but wise and necessary policy of the State, embodied in the Act of 1820. That Act rendered private emancipation impossible. If not done by Legislative authority, it was simply a nullity. Should not all attempts at evasions of the law have been held ineffectual and void? Was not a provision, by deed, or by will, that a slave should be held in nominal servitude, against the plain meaning and intent of the Act?

These cases show that even in a very racist society in which slavery is reserved for one race, some owners will wish to emancipate some slaves. Where manumission is restricted or prohibited by law, some owners will go to considerable lengths to free or attempt to free slaves, frequently supporting their freedom by gifts of property or maintenance. Usually freedom will be granted only for special cause: loyalty by the slave, a sexual relationship between owner and slave, or ties of blood.[45] It seems reasonable to believe that the cases which reached the law reports represent but a small proportion of the attempted manumissions[46] and that many more manumissions would have occurred but for legislation against freeing slaves.

Thus in South Carolina, and no doubt in other states, the free black population before the Civil War would have been larger had not legislation prevented emancipation or the residence of free blacks. And that despite racism.

There is no paradox here. A slaveowner might be thoroughly racist, believe that blacks should be slaves, that manumission should be prohibited or restricted, and that free blacks should be denied the right to remain, and yet fervently wish that some of *his* blacks be treated differently and never be the slaves of another. He may prefer these slaves to be his slaves rather than free, but free rather than the slaves of another. A racist might believe there are exceptions, especially if the exception is his woman or child. He might also reasonably feel obliged to provide support for the former slave upon manumission. The desire of masters to manumit may have been no less in English America than it was in Latin America.

A final word should be said about law and societal concerns in South Carolina. There is no doubt but that often when a government makes law it does so in response to a particular event. The most traumatic event in South Carolina for whites concerning slaves was undoubtedly the Stono uprising of 1739. It was followed in 1740 by the Act for the better Ordering and Governing of Negroes and other Slaves in this Province. This act is comprehensive, and there can be no doubt that it was enacted largely in response to the rebellion. It would be tempting to relate the act's particular rules to the uprising. But things are not that simple. First, such comprehensive legislation had been under discussion for years before the Stono uprising. Second, there was nothing radically new in the act, only a limited tightening of control over slaves. So little in fact is new in the 1740 act that in this chapter mention of it has been almost entirely restricted to the notes, as repeating previous legislation though perhaps with minor modifications.[47]

5

FRANCE AND SLAVE LAW

IN AMERICA

The position was different again for France. Slavery had disappeared from France long before the discovery of the New World.[1] There was no law of slavery. Yet France, like Spain, had undergone a Reception of Roman law, though in a different way. There was no equivalent of *Las Siete Partidas*, and in general there was no one law for France. Instead, for private law France was largely a land of customary law, which varied from place to place. There could be a large area, such as Brittany or Normandy, with a general *coutume*; within it for smaller districts or towns particular *coutumes*. The situation was enormously complicated, but luckily we can make short work of it for our purposes. For law, France can primarily be divided into two parts. The *pays de droit écrit*, territories of written law, lie in the south and largely correspond to the old territories of the Burgundians and the Visigoths. In these, Roman law, the *ius scriptum* or written law, had not been imposed but had been accepted as custom. Therefore in the *pays de droit écrit* the *Corpus Juris* was treated as the law except when there were derogations from it by later custom or legislation. In the *pays de droit coutumier*, territories of customary law, the Reception was not so direct. Roman law had influenced the growth of rules regarded as customary. But when a local custom came to be put into writing, whether unofficially as in the so-called *Coutumiers* or as a result of royal ordinance in the *coutumes*, gaps in the law were often noticed and frequently supplied from Roman law or in terms derived from Roman law. The writing down of the customs was a very slow process but was virtually complete by the middle of the sixteenth century. The *coutumes*, though, were short works and many situations still had to be supplied with law from elsewhere. There was considerable dispute among the scholars and in the various districts as to the proper course of action when a problem arose and the local *coutume* gave no answer. For some scholars, first recourse was to be had to a neighboring custom or the *Coutume de Paris*. For others, recourse was to be had to Roman law. There were three main approaches to this use of Roman law. Some scholars and even some *coutumes* treated Roman law as written law in France; hence it supplemented the customs and was directly applicable when customary law failed to supply an answer. Others claimed that Roman law had authority only because it was written reason and hence, even when custom or legislation failed, it could be made use of only when it was in harmony with the spirit of the custom. A different and powerful approach was to hold that Roman law was the common law of France and the customs were only local variations and therefore had to be interpreted restrictively.[2]

On the subject of slavery, what really matters was that Roman law as it was in Justinian's *Corpus Juris Civilis* was a very potent and continuing source of inspiration in the legal tradition. To develop the law one looked to Roman law. This is nowhere more apparent than in what was probably the most influential French law book for centuries, Jean Domat's *Les Loix civiles dans leur ordre naturel* (first published between 1689 and 1697). Domat's aim was to set out a scheme of Christian law for France, arranged so as to be easily understood. He claims in the first paragraph of his Preface that four kinds of law operate in France. Royal ordinances had authority in all of France. Customs had particular authority within their districts. Roman law was used, he says, in two ways, first, in some places for some matters as custom, second, in all France for some matters, "consisting in this that one observes everywhere these rules of justice and equity that are called 'written reason,' because they are written in Roman law. Thus, for this second use, Roman law has the same authority as have justice and equity on our reason." The fourth source of law in France for Domat was canon law, though he says some of it had been rejected. Not only does Domat give such high authority to Roman law at the outset of his work, but Roman law predominates throughout.

France had no slaves and no law of slavery. France thus acquired slaves in the American possessions before there was a law of slavery. The law of the French overseas possessions was basically the *Coutume de Paris*,[3] which contained nothing on slaves. Nor could recourse be had to other French *coutumes* since they had nothing on slave law either. Given the enormous force of the legal tradition, the inevitable French response was to turn to Roman law. The theory on which Roman law was to be made use of might be obscure,[4] but that would be of less consequence than that there was a practical need for slave law, no slave law existed in France, it was the French practice to look to Roman law to develop private law, and Roman law provided a ready-made model for slave law. Roman law was thus the inevitable model for the French law on slavery.

The French solution to the problem of slave law for the colonies was extensive royal legislation emanating from France, in which Roman law principles predominated. These laws were eventually brought together and published in 1742 in Paris as the *Code noir*.[5] (The two main royal edicts are often individually referred to as the *Code noir*, but for simplicity I shall use the term only for the published book of 1742.) The French approach was thus artificial in at least two ways. First, the law was not made on the spot where the local conditions and needs were in front of the eyes of the legislator, but far away in the very different circumstances of Paris. Second, the law was then made by lawyers trained in Roman law and accustomed to use it to develop the law. And social conditions in ancient Rome were not those of French America. Still, since the French were legislating for a new situation, it is not surprising that they innovated by giving a public dimension to slave law. For example, the fixed penalty of death was enacted for a slave who struck his master, his mistress, her husband, or their children on the face so as to bruise or cause bleeding.[6] The significant point is that this public dimension was far less marked than it was in English America.

One aspect of legal development in this way may be mentioned at the outset. In France, in contrast to Spain, no law of slavery developed from Roman law before slave law was needed for the colonies. Hence there was no progression from Roman law such as exists in *Las Siete Partidas* 4.21.6 allowing a slave to bring an action against the owner who cruelly mistreated him (instead of, as at Rome, fleeing to a statue of the emperor or a shrine). And in the French colonies, in contrast to those of Spain, slaves never had such a right.

The use made of Roman law in the *Code noir* is well exemplified by article 37 of the royal edict of March 1685 for the French American islands.[7] Roman law had allowed a *paterfamilias* or owner who was sued for a private wrong (including theft) committed by his son or slave or injury caused by his animal to pay the amount of the suit or, if he preferred, surrender the offending person or animal.[8] Noxal surrender, as it is called, was not received in France, not even for animals. But article 37 allowed noxal surrender of slaves, at the option of the owner, for their thefts or other wrongs.[9] A similar provision occurs in article 31 of the royal edict of March 1724 for Louisiana.[10]

What concerns us most, though, is manumission. Article 55 of the edict of March 1685 states: "Owners who are twenty years old can free their slaves by any act *inter vivos* or *mortis causa* without being bound to give a reason for the manumission, and without needing parental consent even if they are under twenty-five."[11] And article 56 says: "Children [sic. But the article should read 'Slaves'] who have been made universal legatees by their masters or named as executors of their wills or tutors of their children will be held and reputed, and we so hold and regard them, as freedmen."[12] Article 57[13] gives freed slaves French citizenship automatically even if they were not born in the French islands. The role of Roman law in determining the basic import of these rules is obvious, just as it is, for example, in article 58,[14] which requires freedmen to show "un respect singulier" to their former owners just as Roman freedmen owed *obsequium* to their patrons.[15]

Very similar provisions are to be found in the royal edict of March 1724 regulating slavery in Louisiana. Article 50 allows owners over age twenty-five to free their slaves *inter vivos* or *mortis causa*, but the permission of the Conseil Supérieur is required though it will be granted without charge if the masters' motives are legitimate. The requirement of the Conseil's permission is expressly said to be needed because some masters may be so mercenary as to make slaves pay to be free, which drives them to theft and brigandage.[16] The same complaint was voiced by Dionysius of Halicarnassus for first-century Rome. This provision does not seem to have been intended to operate in a concealed way to make manumission in general more difficult, other than is expressed. The records of the Conseil Supérieur have been examined, and it appears that the right to manumit was freely granted. A frequent reason for manumission was "good and faithful service."[17] One should not be surprised that in Spanish colonies official consent to manumission was not required, but in French Louisiana it was. France had no slaves, but the French had a precedent for their practice. Serfdom had long remained in some parts of France such as Nivernais, Troyes, Bourbonnais, Meaux, Bourgogne, Vitry, Chaumont en Bassigny, Châlons, and la Marche, and this is reflected in the *coutumes*.[18] When a landowner wished to release his serfs from the land, he had to obtain the permission of the king.[19] Article 51 of this code for Louisiana grants freedom to slaves whose masters by will appoint them guardians to their children.[20] The article says nothing, though, about slaves appointed as heirs by their masters since the following article, 52, forbids gifts to be made by whites to their freedmen or to free blacks, whether *inter vivos* or *mortis causa*. Such gifts are void and are to be applied for the benefit of the nearest hospital.[21] The very existence of the provision indicates that the lawmakers believe that, without it, such gifts would be made. The same article gives freedmen French citizenship even if they were not born in Louisiana. Article 53 commands that freedmen show their former owners "un respect singulier."[22]

The Catholic view of marriage meant that there could be no parallel to Justinian's rule in C.6.4.4.3 that if an owner had no wife and made his slave woman his concubine, and she remained in that condition at his death, the slave woman become free and their children were freeborn. There is, however, a resounding echo of this rule in the second part of article 9 of the edict of March 1685. The first part of article 9 declared that free men who had a child or children from concubinage with their slaves,[23] and masters who permitted this, would each be condemned in a fine of two thousand pounds of sugar, and if they were owners of the slave woman in question, they would, in addition, be deprived of the slave and the children, who would be confiscated for the benefit of the hospital and could never be freed. The latter part of article 9 reads: "We do not, however, intend the present article to take effect when the man was not married to another person during his concubinage with his slave, and marries in the forms prescribed by the church the said slave who thereby becomes freed, and the children made free and legitimate."[24] A very similar provision is in article 6 of the edict of March 1724 for Louisiana.[25]

Likewise, there were restrictions on the masters' rights to punish. Article 42 of the edict of March 1685 for the islands allows masters who think their slaves merit it to put their slaves in chains and to beat them with rods or whips but not to torture them or mutilate a limb under penalty (among other things) of confiscation of the slave.[26] A provision to similar effect appears in article 38 of the edict of March 1724.[27] But just as in Roman law, so in article 31 of the edict of March 1685 for the islands legal personality is denied to slaves to the extent that they cannot be parties either as plaintiff or defendant in any civil action, or be the civil party in any criminal action, or in a criminal matter seek reparation for any outrage or excess committed against them.[28]

Article 25 of the edict of March 1724 is to much the same effect.[29] Article 30 of the edict of March 1685 limits the value of slave testimony. When slaves are heard in evidence, their depositions serve only as an account to aid the judge in seeking enlightenment elsewhere, but from the evidence no presumption nor conjecture nor the slightest iota of proof is to be drawn. The corresponding article 24 of the edict of March 1724 is to rather different effect.[30] Slaves in both civil and criminal cases cannot be witnesses unless they are necessary witnesses and only in the absence of white witnesses; and in no case can they be witnesses for or against their master.

Punishment of criminal slaves included branding, cutting off of ears, hamstringing, and death.[31] When a slave was executed, his value was first estimated and the price given to the master.[32]

Article 44 of the edict of March 1685 goes so far in treating slaves as chattels that it declares them to be movables. This has legal effects; for instance, they become part of the marital community property.[33] A similar provision is in article 40 of the edict of March 1724.[34]

French slaves, like Roman slaves, could have a *peculium*, a point that emerges in a striking way from article 23 of the edict of March 1724, which is particularly significant for Roman influence. Article 22 had declared that slaves could own nothing and all their acquisitions belonged to their masters.[35] Article 23 reads:

> We wish nonetheless that masters be bound by what their slaves did by their order, together with what they have managed and traded in their shops, and for the particular type of business their masters put them in charge of; and in the event that their masters gave them no orders and did not put them in charge, they will be liable only for an amount equal to what has been turned to their profit; and if nothing has profited the masters, the *peculium* of the said slaves, which the masters allowed them to have, will be liable after the masters have preferentially deducted what was due to them: except that where the *peculium* consisted in whole or in part of goods in which the slaves had authority to trade separately, the masters will come in only by contribution for one *sol* in the *livre* with the other creditors.[36]

These rules very much correspond to the Roman so-called *actiones adiecticiae qualitatis*, which were given against a father or owner on account of contractual arrangements made by a son or slave. Thus the *actio quod iussu* lay for up to the full amount of any transaction authorized by the *paterfamilias*. The *actio institoria* lay when one person used another to run a business. The *actio de peculio et in rem verso* lay for up to the amount by which the *paterfamilias* had profited and up to the amount of the *peculium*. The *peculium* was calculated after deduction from it of any debts due by the son or slave to the *paterfamilias*. The more complicated *actio tributoria* lay if a son or slave, with the knowledge of the *paterfamilias*, traded with his *peculium* or part of it, up to the limit of that part of the *peculium*, and the *paterfamilias* had no right to deduct any debt owed to him.

The slaves' humanity, though not their legal personality, is recognized by laws relating to their Christian faith,[37] by laws giving validity to their marriages[38] and forbidding husband, wife, and young children to be sold separately,[39] and by laws imposing duties on masters to feed, clothe, house, and otherwise look after them.[40]

These laws are similar to those in the Spanish colonies and do not require extensive discussion. It is of interest, though, that, since by article 1 of the edict of March 1685 there could be no Jewish colonists, there was no need for a provision, corresponding to Roman and Spanish law, forbidding Jews to have Christian slaves.

I have left to the end one particular aspect of manumission. A royal ordinance of 24 October 1713[41] for the French islands forbade, for reasons that it gave, masters to free their slaves without first having obtained written permission from the governors, intendants, or *commissaires ordonnateurs*. It also ordered that manumissions performed without these permissions were void and that the slaves so freed should be sold for the profit of His Majesty. A further royal ordinance for the islands of 15 June 1736[42] records that masters are disobeying the ordinance and that, moreover, there are others who are having children baptized as free whose mothers are slaves. (This latter practice smacks of a manumittory dodge by owners, akin to *manumissio vindicta* at Rome.) The ordinance then commands the enforcement of the ordinance of 1713 and forbids priests to baptize any children as free unless the manumission of the mother, with the proper written permission, is first proved.

From our perspective it is interesting enough that restrictions were placed on the masters' freedom to manumit slaves. What is still more interesting is that the ordinance of 1736 shows that the restrictions were being evaded. And it takes little imagination to believe that the babies who were being freed (by baptism as free) and whose mothers were their owners' slaves were the children or grandchildren of the manumitting owners. It is also, no doubt, significant that Berquin Duvallon, reporting on his visit to Louisiana in 1802, stated that there were more free mulattoes than free blacks.[43] The manumission by masters of their slave concubines was also well known in the French Antilles.[44] The situation in South Carolina will be recalled.

6

PORTUGAL AND SLAVE LAW

IN AMERICA

The situation in Portugal and the Portuguese colonies was again different. The *Visigothic Code* with its rules on slavery would appear to have applied, but after the Reconquista there seem to have been no more slaves except Moorish captives.[1] Various municipal *forais,* collections of town law, from the twelfth century contain regulations on slaves, but they had little impact on later developments. By the fourteenth century black slaves were becoming common,[2] but towns ceased to regulate slavery, and regulation was left to royal legislation.[3]

When the American colonies were incorporated into the kingdom by the doctrine of *accessio*, the main laws of Portugal which were applicable were the *Ordenaçoes Filipinas*. These were ordinances begun by Philip I and promulgated by Philip II for Portugal under Spanish domination and confirmed by a law of the Portuguese king, João IV in 1643. They remained in force for over three centuries, continuing even after Brazil became independent in 1822. The *Ordenaçoes* are divided into five books of which the fourth deals with private law. Title 64 of book 3 reads:

Whenever any case is brought before a court, which is governed by any law of our kingdoms or practice of our court or long observed custom in the said kingdoms or in any part of them and which by law ought to be observed, such case shall be decided by them, notwithstanding that the Imperial Laws [i.e., the *Corpus Juris Civilis*] dispose in a different way with regard to the said case. Because wherever a law, practice, or custom of our kingdoms makes provisions, all other laws and rights cease to apply. And when the case which is referred to is not decided by law, practice, or custom of our kingdoms we command that it be decided, in matter which involves sin, by the Holy Canons.

And in matter which does not involve sin it is to be decided by the Imperial Laws although the Holy Canons determine otherwise. These Imperial Laws we order to be observed only on account of good reason on which they are based. 1. And if the case which is before the court is not decided by a law of our kingdoms, practice, or custom as above said, or by the Imperial Laws or by the Holy Canons, then we order the glosses of Accursius which are incorporated in the said Laws to be observed when they are not disapproved by the common opinion of the Doctors; and when by the said glosses the case is not decided, then following the opinion of Bartolus because his opinion generally conforms to reason notwithstanding that some Doctors held the contrary, unless the common opinion of the Doctors who wrote after him was to the contrary. 2. And on the occurrence of a case which is provided for in none of the said ways we order that we be notified so that we may decide it. For not only are such determinations a judgment on such facts as are treated in the case, but they are laws for determining other similar cases. 3. And when the case which is involved is such that it is not a matter of sin and was not decided by a law of the kingdom, nor the practice of our court, nor custom of our kingdoms, nor the Imperial Law, and it was decided by the texts of the Canons in one way and by the glosses and Doctors of the laws in another way, we order that such case be remitted to us so that we give our decision upon it, which will be followed.[4]

From an early date the *Ordenações Filipinas* were considered to be badly drafted, with many gaps, and to represent the spirit of the Middle Ages in modern times.[5] But of importance here is that, though the *Ordenações Filipinas* treat slavery as an everyday matter, very few provisions lay down the law. *Ordenações Filipinas* 5.36.1 does, however, allow owners only moderate physical punishment of their slaves. In this regard, slaves are expressly placed on a level with servants, pupils, wives, or children. The relationship with *Las Siete Partidas* 7.8.9 is readily apparent. Again, in harmony with Roman law, *Ordenações Filipinas* 4.17 allows those who buy slaves or beasts to reject them for disease or defects.[6] The use of the double terminology for the grounds of rejection, "doenças ou manqueiras," recalls the Roman *morbus vitiumve*.[7] Apart from a few such provisions there was no statutory slave law (except possibly that in the

Visigothic Code, which does not seem to have been used). Nor apparently did the courts much use custom to regulate slave law. Hence the Roman law of Justinian's *Corpus Juris Civilis* was directly relevant and was the main authority for the law of slavery. If that source did not provide a solution, recourse would be had to the Accursian gloss, failing which the opinion of Bartolus would prevail, unless the general opinion of the doctors was against him. Philip II and Philip III also, in laws of 1597 and 1612, proscribed the new (humanist) learning of Cujas and approved the writings of Bartolus.[8] Thus, when the colonies were incorporated into Portugal, and slaves were introduced into them, there was already slave law and that law was primarily Roman law.

The *Ordenaçoes Filipinas* were modified on 18 August 1769 by the *Lei da Boa Razão* (the Law of Sound Reason). Scholars regard this as a great step forward in the evolution of Portuguese private law.[9] It gave authority and the force of law to the established practice of the Casa da Supplicação. The decisions of the senates of Portugal, Bahia, Rio de Janeiro, and the Indies were not to have the force of law unless they were confirmed by the Casa da Supplicação (Section 8). By section 9 Roman law was to cease to be subsidiary law. Instead, recourse was to be had to the perpetual and immutable principles of natural law and the universal rules of the *ius gentium* and to the economic, political, and mercantile laws of the more advanced nations. Section 11 approved only those interpretations of statute which could be derived from the reasons for passing the law, the occasion, and the spirit of the law. Section 10 declared it to be an error to regard Portuguese statutory law as agreeing with the *ius commune*. Section 13 forbade reference to Accursius, Bartolus, and other Doctors. The final section, 14, gave the force of law to custom only if it was reasonable, not contrary to written law, and had been followed for a century by the courts.

Thus, technically, in 1769, the *Lei de Boa Razão* abolished the rule of Roman law. But much Roman law had already been injected into slave law by decisions before 1769 in the courts of the Portuguese kingdoms and by long-established custom. The *ius commune*, though it was much based on Roman law, might have ended slavery altogether. For in the European territories such as Germany and the Netherlands, where *ius commune* was most influential, slavery did not exist. Yet the statute declared that the *ius commune* was not the same as Portuguese law. Portuguese statutes were to be interpreted only according to their own spirit. But little new legislation was forthcoming. What the law on slavery was going to be (apart from Portuguese legislation), would then depend primarily on the senses attributed to natural law and the law of nations. It must be stressed that the *Lei da Boa Razão* did not directly add to the substantive law, which on slavery, as on other matters, was very thin.

The very potent concept of natural law has had a long history and has undergone many transformations. Its basic premise is that the validity or otherwise of law is not to be decided by human promulgation but by some intrinsic standard. A powerful movement (which one might call the Law of Reason) in the seventeenth and eighteenth centuries sought to make natural law independent of (though not divorced from) theological underpinnings. On this approach one can say generally that natural law comprises the rules that can be uncovered by the use of reason to enable humans—who are social animals—to live peacefully in society. The very name of the statute, *Lei da Boa Razão*, shows that this is the sense to be attributed to its usage of natural law. One must then at once observe that at this date scholars did not necessarily think slavery was contrary to natural law in this sense. Thus the influential Ulrich Huber (1636–94) of Friesland in his *Praelectiones Juris Civilis* on the *Institutes* 1.3 states:

> As we just said, slavery is not necessarily at odds with reason. For the Christians themselves only late disapproved of slavery, nor is it disapproved of in the Old or New Testament. Likewise laws of Charlemagne, Louis the Pious, and Lothar on slaves survive in the *Laws of Charlemagne and the Lombards*. Indeed, there exist rulings of King William of Sicily and of the Emperor Frederick on runaway slaves in *Neopolitan Decisions*. But from that time, that is 1212 A.D. or not much later, Christians stopped enslaving one another, which is also the case among the Muslims and Turks according to Busbequius,

Letter 3, where he also argues that slavery was not rightly removed from among us. The specious pretext of charitableness was adduced, but in vain. The result was a flood of free persons whom wantonness and need drove to wickedness or beggary. The ministrations of the enlarged family were reduced. Add that slaughter in war became more frequent when slavery was removed, which the Romans put to the test in civil wars in which the captives were not made slaves. Tacitus, *Histories* 2, cap. 44, Plutarch, *Otho*, and D.49.15.21.1. This reasoning is not without weight. See Berneggerus on Tacitus, *Germania*, question 134.[10]

Huber was not, of course, authoritative for the Portuguese, but in this opinion he was by no means isolated. And lest the quotation be used to his discredit, it should be mentioned that elsewhere in a less well-known work, Huber wrote of his disapproval of slavery as it was practiced in America.[11]

The general course of theoretical development here is easily traced. Theological discussion had given a meaning to natural law very different from that assigned to it in the Roman sources, where it was the law that applied equally to all other animals as well as to humans. Perhaps on this account the Roman notion of natural law was often discarded by jurists on the basis that it was not law at all but instinct. Natural law was then claimed to be the same as, or coextensive with, or closely connected to, the *ius gentium*.[12] Since the Roman texts had stated that slavery was an institution of the *ius gentium*, some scholars could now claim it was in accordance with natural law.[13]

Perhaps more relevant for natural law and *ius gentium* in Portuguese America was J. C. Heineccius (1681–1741). His numerous writings on law were among the most popular of the eighteenth century. Thus his *Elementa juris civilis*, on Roman law, was probably the influential work most used in Latin America. His work on natural law and the *ius gentium*, *Elementa juris naturae et gentium*, was translated several times into Spanish (as well as into French and Italian) and was published even in Ayacucho in Peru in 1832. Heineccius deals with natural law in book 1 and *ius gentium* in book 2. He defines natural law as "the complex of laws promulgated by immortal God himself to humankind through right reason."[14] Of *ius gentium* he says:

> Since, moreover, the law of nature embraces the laws which were promulgated to the whole humankind through right reason, but men can be considered either as individuals or as they are combined into certain societies; therefore, the law by which the actions of individuals are ruled is *natural*; that which in societies and between societies teaches what is just and what unjust we call *ius gentium* and so the precepts and legal rule of both sorts of law are the same; and indeed *ius gentium* is itself natural law applied to the social human life, to the transactions of societies and whole nations.[15]

On this basis, the issue facing scholars was to build up a system of law (that could be accepted in practice) not on the basis of existing legal rules or systems but that could be deduced by reasoning about the nature of man as a social animal.

But as no one is free from his culture, so no lawyer is free from his legal culture, and a common pattern inevitably emerged in European writings on natural law. Basic legal institutions such as ownership, contract, or marriage are accepted or argued for as "natural." Then the details are worked out. But in the legal culture of the day, the basic legal institutions had derived from Roman law. The details that could be worked out—given the preconceptions of the scholars—were thus largely from Roman law. But jurists did have the opportunity, in an apparently rational way, of discarding points of Roman law, which in any event had not been received. Two examples will serve as illustrations of the results. First, the Romans gave an action to someone who without authorization acted on behalf of another, when he intended to act for that person and not himself, and when it was reasonable for him to do so. The action was to compensate the actor for any loss or expense he might incur, but only up to the amount of the benefit he conferred at the time of acting. This institution of *negotiorum gestio*, with many of its Roman details, was accepted by Heineccius at 1.13.348 as part of natural law. It existed (and exists) in legal systems which derived from Roman law but is so foreign to systems not so derived (and, perhaps one could claim, to natural law) that no equivalent existed in English law. Second, Heineccius argues at 1.9.235 that originally all things were held in common when there was enough for everyone, but with time there came to be not enough to go round and hence of necessity the concept of ownership was introduced. Accordingly, since ownership is necessary, it must be natural. Then in subsequent sections Heineccius deals with the ways in which ownership is acquired, and these are based on Roman law. But there can be minor differences. Thus, in Roman law, *traditio*, which was the basic way of transferring ownership upon agreement, required actual physical delivery in the standard case. This requirement was not accepted in Heineccius's day, and he says of it, "It is scarcely probable that natural law and the *jus gentium* would approve this subtlety, as Grotius and Puffendorf rightly observe."[16]

Heineccius accepts slavery as part of the *ius gentium* and then proceeds to build up a law of slavery.[17] For example, the foundation of slavery is ownership, hence that ownership must be acquired by good title. Outside of marriage (which, he says, can scarcely apply to slaves), the offspring follows the condition of the mother. For both of these propositions Heineccius cites as authority his arguments on natural law on the acquisition of ownership. The result for Heineccius is that the child of a slave woman follows the status of the mother, as if as an accessory to her, with the consequence that the child belongs to the mother's owner. In similar fashion, he argues, for instance, that the owner has free disposition of his slaves[18] and that he can free slaves.[19]

We need follow Heineccius no further. Though influential, he was never authoritative in Portugal or her colonies. What concerns us is that the *Lei da Boa Razão* declared that, in the absence of statute, the law was to be *ius naturale* and *ius gentium*; that these ideal systems were built up in large measure on the basic principles of Roman law; and that slavery could be accepted as part of these ideal systems by jurists like Huber and Heineccius. But in applying *ius naturale* and *ius gentium* to actual cases, courts had to face a fundamental problem. What exactly was this law? In the first place, scholars frequently disagreed. Second, in the nature of things, accounts of these systems could never be detailed enough to provide answers to actual problems. The solution of the courts was to make much use of Roman law.[20]

As one might expect in the light of the foregoing, accounts of slave law in Brazil are replete with references to Roman law.[21] In Roman law, slaves could not marry. The Roman Catholic church recognized slave marriages as valid, and though the laws of the church were tacitly accepted in Brazil, there were almost no effects of this recognition in the civil law.[22] But the owner could not sell or alienate a slave in such a way that he or she could not continue the matrimonial life.[23]

Two details of the law in Portuguese America are particularly revealing. A slave who was freed could ransom his wife and children. And if a free man voluntarily subjected himself to slavery, accompanying his slave wife and children, they all acquired freedom on the death of the owner.[24] These rather liberal rules have no parallel in Roman law or apparently anywhere else in America. How, then, is their existence to be explained, especially because Portugal and Portuguese America were not noted for innovations in private law? The answer is that the laws of a Byzantine emperor, Leo the Wise, who ruled from 886 to 912, came to be included in some editions of the *Corpus Juris Civilis* and in Brazil, at least, were treated as part of Roman law. The legal rules just described are contained in Leo's constitutions 100 and 101. The rules were accepted in Brazil, therefore, on the basis that they were part of the *Corpus Juris Civilis*.

The slave was not a legal person, hence in private law could not be a party to an action, whether as plaintiff or defendant. There were exceptions, though, in spiritual matters such as marriage, actions concerning the slave's freedom, and actions involving obvious public interest. Likewise, *Ordenações Filipinas* 3.56.3 declared for private law that a slave could not be a witness or examined except in the cases where the law so expressly declared. *Ordenações Filipinas* 4.85 *pr.* declared that a slave could not be a witness to a will unless he was thought to be free when the will was made and only subsequently was seen to be a slave, did not take anything under the will, and by common error was generally reputed to be free. This is very much in line with Roman law as set out in *J.2.10.7.* From Roman law it was also accepted that when a slave could be a witness, his testimony was allowable only if the truth could be discovered in no other way[25] and only after he had been tortured.[26]

The law of manumission by the owner was the law of Rome. There were few restrictions, and they were the familiar ones such as to prevent fraud against creditors, or to avoid prejudice to the *herdeiros necessários.*[27] Manumission did not require any particular formalities,[28] the common ways being in writing, by will or codicil, or by baptism. At baptism, freedom resulted only if the owner showed this was his intention.[29]

Though writers at times show an inclination to believe that slaves could own property, including even other slaves and money—and hence could buy their freedom—what was in operation was in fact a system of *peculium* deriving from the Roman model. The owner allowed the slave to keep control of a proportion of what he gained, though in law this belonged to the slaveowner.

Few slaves were actually freed. It appears that in the cities of Rio, Salvador, and Paraty (which are the only ones so far investigated), freed slaves made up no more than 0.5 percent or 2 percent of the population.[30]

Only those slaves were freed who could pay for it, and far more women then men were freed. The calculations of S. M. De Q. Mattoso indicate that approximately twice as many women as men were freed, yet in the slave population as a whole men were twice as numerous as women.[31] This bears out the conclusion when dealing with Roman slaves that the intimacy of the relationship between owner and slave was an important factor influencing manumission. Many of the freed women will have been concubines of the owner. Until 1745,[32] the percentage of freed children was high. Some were manumitted at the instigation of godparents, and others will have been the children of the owner. Slaves of mixed race were freed much more frequently than were blacks.[33]

As in Rome, slavery might end even against the wishes of the owner, but the law in Brazil came to be more generous (from the slave's perspective). A slave who found a diamond larger than twenty carats was freed by the state, which compensated the owner. A slave was also freed if he denounced his owner for smuggling or dealing in goods in which the government had a monopoly, namely gold, diamonds, and Brazil wood.[34]

If one may judge from individual instances, important changes were occurring late in the history of the law. By *Avisos* 2 of 17 March and 29 July 1830 freedom was to be conferred on a female slave who had offered a price for her freedom. And likewise by *Aviso* 3 of 15 December 1831 freedom was to be conferred against an owner who demanded an exorbitant price for manumission of a female slave.[35] A system was arising akin to the Spanish *coartación*.

As we have seen, only moderate punishment by the owner of the slave was permitted even by the *Ordenaçoes Filipinas*.[36] The owner could only punish a slave, as a father a son, or a master a servant. It is important that the rule was established before Brazil became a colony. If a master was vicious, the law authorized a slave to request that the owner sell him.[37] Security might be required of an owner who was proved to have mistreated a slave.[38] Yet owners were permitted to mutilate slaves until 1824. A regulation of 1830 prohibited administering more than fifty lashes of the whip at any one time. (As a result, punishment might be spread over a long period). The use of the whip was abolished in 1886.[39]

The punishment of slaves at criminal law started from a Roman basis with some cruel penalties evident in the *Ordenaçoes Filipinas*. Thus runaways could be tortured to make statements,[40] and they could suffer mutilation of the body for killing their owner or his son.[41] Subsequent rules introduced in the eighteenth century allowed branding with a hot iron.[42] But in the imperial constitution of 1824, torture, branding, and cruel punishments in general were prohibited.[43] Whipping was also abolished.[44]

The freed slave owned respect to his patron. To bring suit against his patron, the freedman had to get authorization from the court. A freedman could be reenslaved for ingratitude.[45]

The Brazilian constitution of 1815 declared that a freed slave who had been born in Brazil was a citizen by birth, but others had to undergo a naturalization process, which was the same as that for foreigners who wished to become citizens. There were severe limitations on the public law rights of freed slaves.[46]

There is a widely held belief that slaves were better treated in the Portuguese colonies than elsewhere in America. Conclusions are then drawn on this basis. Above all, it is argued that the Portuguese male was less sexually conservative than other slaveowners, was more drawn to African women, and hence was less racially discriminatory.[47] I have no desire to go into the debate, but there is considerable evidence against the belief that slaves were better treated in Brazil than elsewhere.[48] Indeed, it can be argued that slaves were worse treated in Brazil than elsewhere.[49]

7

SLAVE LAW

IN DUTCH AMERICA

Since this book deals with slave law only in areas where slavery flourished as a social and economic institution, I will say nothing of slave law in the New Netherlands colony. Thus the slave law to be investigated is that found in the Caribbean and Surinam. Of all systems of slavery in America, the slave law in Dutch America seems the least approachable,[1] so much so that there is little reference to it in accounts of the social institutions of slavery. This is in marked contrast to the discussions of slavery in the colonies of the other European powers. For the Dutch possessions, modern writers do not seem to draw conclusions from the state of the law to the state of society. Moreover, I have found no secondary literature directly on slave law in Dutch America. The probable explanation, as will appear incidentally, lies in the nature of the sources of law.

The charter to the Dutch West India Company (gheoctroyeerde West-Indische Compagnie) was granted by the States-General of the Netherlands on 3 June 1621.[2] The charter did not grant the company power to legislate and did not state what the law was to be in the territories the company colonized. A *placaat* of 13 October 1629, *Ordre van Regieringe in West-Indien*, provided in article 56 that in private law actions, personal or real, the law to be applied was the common law of the United Provinces or such of it as should be approved by the Council of Nineteen—another name for the governing body of the company—but the procedure was to be as short as possible according to the nature of the case.[3] Thus the law to be applied in general by the company was not that specific to any one province, but the common law of the United Provinces, and the company was given power to refuse to apply part of that law. But it was not expressly given power to legislate. In practice, the company did issue numerous *placaaten*, and the States-General also issued *placaaten* relating to the company's territories.

Roman law had been received in the United Provinces but to differing degrees in the different provinces. Friesland had been most open to the Reception, but Holland had also been deeply penetrated, though to a lesser extent. Other provinces such as Groningen, Gelderland, Overijssel, and Drente were much less affected.[4] The most important contemporary law books concentrated on Holland and Friesland. But the provinces had in common an absence of slavery and of slave law. How, then, was this law to develop in Dutch America? Not only was there no existing law in the home country in the seventeenth century, but the American possessions were not colonies of the home government, but under the control of a trading company, with a local governor and council. The company would be primarily interested in looking after its affairs with little concern otherwise in controlling the behavior of colonists.

The Dutch had no slave law. Since the territories controlled by the West Indian Company were not colonies of the United Provinces, the States-General would not and did not issue systematic or comprehensive legislation. In fact, the States-General issued very few *placaaten* which concerned slaves in the company's colonies and none of these is of general significance. They are all concerned with specific events.[5] Thus slavery was introduced into the Dutch American possessions without a law of slavery; and the Dutch government, the States-General, did not thereafter create a law of slavery. Although colonists were admitted, the territories were controlled by the trading company and, in the nature of things, its lawmaking would be largely restricted to keeping the peace and preserving its revenues. It is not surprising that what law was created afresh had a public dimension with a superficial resemblance to that of English America. Moreover, there was no appropriate available model to provide law in books. The Portuguese in America could—at least in theory—go straight to the *Corpus Juris Civilis* to supply their needs. But Roman slave law had not been received in the United Provinces. The law attributed to the West India Company's possessions was the common law of the United Provinces (insofar as it was appropriate), hence the law in books was to be found in the books on Roman-Dutch law,[6] or on the law of Holland[7] or of Friesland.[8] And these books, when they were available and used, habitually did not set out a law of slavery, Roman or otherwise.

Where, then, was the law found? The major part of the answer is to be found in a misuse or misunderstanding of article 61 of the *placaat* of 13 October 1629. A few paragraphs that follow article 56 (which has already been mentioned) deal with matters of procedure and particular topics such as marriage, succession, and transfer of land. Then comes article 61: "In other matters of contracts of all kinds and trading the common written laws should be followed."[9] It must be correct to take "de gemeene beschreven Rechten" ("the common written laws") as meaning or including Roman law. First, Roman law is frequently referred to as the written law. Second, Dutch common law as set out by jurists was not considered written law. However important their works were, they were not statutes, which, including the *Corpus Juris Civilis*, were alone considered written laws. Third, the Roman law of contracts was particularly well developed. But the problem is that slave law is not mentioned expressly in any of the provisions of the *placaat* of 13 October 1629 and does not appear to fall under the wording of article 61. That makes Roman law apply to all kinds of contracts and trading, and this is reasonable given that the Roman law of contracts was so highly developed. But nothing would seem to justify the extension of application of article 61 to slave law, though we know that it was so extended. In fact, that article 61 did apply to slave law was expressly declared by the Hof van Holland in a case decided on 23 March 1736 and upheld by the Hooge Raad on 3 July 1736. A slave who had run away and escaped by ship from Curaçao was claimed by his female owner in Amsterdam, and the courts held that Roman law applied in Curaçao and the runaway remained a slave. Cornelius van Bynkershoek, reporting the case, states:

> Slavery exists in Curaçao, and this is a colony under the auspices and government of the States-General. There, with a few exceptions, Ro-

man law flourishes by §61 of the *placaat* which the States-General laid down to the West India Company on 13 October 1629 (*Plac.* 2, p. 1235). Therefore, the laws on slaves are in force, and whatever is laid down about runaway slaves in the whole title of the *Digest* and *Code* on runaway slaves.[10]

The opinion of Gudelinus in his *De Jure Novissimo* 1.4, which was followed by other jurists, that a runaway slave who entered a territory where slavery did not exist became free, was disallowed on the basis that it applied only to a slave coming from another kingdom.

The case is certainly not the first from the United Provinces to discuss slave law in Dutch America; indeed, Bynkershoek refers in his report to an earlier case. But apart from a statement in J. van der Linden showing that it was accepted in the United Provinces that a runaway slave from a Dutch territory remained a slave,[11] I have found no other juristic opinion or judicial decision, earlier or later, on the subject.[12] As reported, the courts simply accepted that article 61 applied to the law of slavery. A possible explanation is that "In andere saecken" ("in other matters"), was taken to mean that, apart from the particular topics set out in the preceding articles, Roman law generally applied. Or perhaps because "van allerley Contracten ende handelingen" ("of contracts of all kinds and trading") was treated as "of contracts above all, and trading." Or perhaps because "handeling" ("trading") was treated as covering all aspects of the law relating to things, such as slaves, which were traded. None of these interpretations of article 61 is tenable, but the fact remains that some such misuse of article 61—presumably deliberate—was needed to make the article applicable to the law of slavery. In the absence of further evidence, the conclusion is presumably justified that the Dutch, simply because of their legal cultural heritage, would inevitably make Roman law the basis of their slave law.

This was the approach taken in Holland to the colonial slave law in the Dutch American territories, and it is the best evidence that the law in force in the territories was Roman law.[13] But the West India Company did issue *placaaten* on the subject. Theoretically, these probably were not law, but in practice the local courts would give weight to them. (When in discussing a *placaat* I use the terms *blacks* or *mulattoes* without specifying whether they were free or slaves, I am reflecting an imprecision in the *placaat* itself.)

For convenience, these *placaaten* of the Dutch West India Company may artificially be divided into groups. A first grouping can be of those *placaaten* which particularly bring out the public law dimension. Thus we find *placaaten* instructing owners to deliver up a number of slaves to perform an amount of public work;[14] restricting slaves from drumming, dancing, or going out (particularly on Sundays or in particular places);[15] restricting fishing or traveling on rivers or being on boats (sometimes unless in the presence of whites);[16] establishing a minimum proportion of whites to slaves on plantations;[17] setting out rules to hinder the running away, arming, and hiding of slaves;[18] establishing penalties (even of death) for runaways;[19] forbidding the selling of gunpowder or shot to slaves;[20] regulating the behavior of whites (in trading or gambling) with slaves;[21] regulating decent and respectable behavior of slaves;[22] regulating the movement of slaves (and sometimes of free blacks), for example, by restricting their access to certain places or requiring written passes;[23] registering the markings of slaves;[24] fixing rewards for catchers of slaves;[25] setting up and running a fund to meet the costs of coping with runaways;[26] forbidding slaves to be worked on Sundays;[27] fixing minimum standards of caring for slaves;[28] forbidding assemblies of slaves;[29] forbidding the sale of diseased slaves;[30] providing for a census[31] and taxing[32] of slaves. Each *placaat* was, of course, issued for a particular colony, and which rules applied varied from place to place.

A second convenient grouping is of *placaaten* that restrict trading by or with slaves. Thus for Curaçao a *placaat* of 1710 forbade inhabitants from letting their slaves sell on the street anything other than greens, fruit, meat, fish, or other eatables.[33] The reason expressly given is to restrict the sale of stolen property. In 1742, inhabitants were told to refrain from renting their houses or other immovables to slaves, and any such contracts were to be unenforceable.[34] The reason given is that questions and differences arise daily over such renting to or by negroes or mulattoes who actually are slaves. In 1769 a *placaat* forbade the buying or taking in pledge of gold or silver work from negroes or mulattoes without a letter from the owner or sheriff's deputy.[35] When the black was a slave, the letter was to be from his owner or the owner of the goods, showing that the slave was charged with the sale or pledge. When the black was free, the letter was to be from the deputy sheriff, showing that the black was free and had shown his right to ownership. This *placaat*, too, was expressly to prevent theft.

These three *placaaten* from Curaçao represent very limited re-strictions on trading by or with slaves. The first and third are intended to restrict theft by inhibiting the sale of stolen goods. Yet the first does allow masters to have their slaves sell in the street precisely those things that one would expect slaves to sell for their master. And the third does not prohibit sales and pledges of gold and silver work by slaves and free blacks, but only demands that they have written proof of their authority to sell. The second illuminates other aspects of slave law. Hiring of houses to blacks caused problems because of the difficulty of distinguishing free from slave,[36] and the *placaat* forbids leasing of houses to slaves, though not to free blacks. Thus it puts the onus on those who hire out houses to determine the status of those blacks they deal with. Again, it is surely not prohibiting hiring houses to those slaves who are simply acting as agents of their owner. Hence it indicates both that slaves could have a *peculium* to deal with and that they might lease a house for themselves, not their owner, to live in. The daily problems then referred to in the *placaat* were that some slaves rented houses on their own account without having a sufficient *peculium*.

The story for St. Maarten is similar. A *placaat* of 1773[37] (after relating that *placaaten* of 1752, 1754, and 1768 had properly for-bidden inhabitants to send out slaves to trade in bread or other provisions, sugar, or cotton without a written authorization specify-ing everything expressly) states that trading in alcohol is again being practiced. A first provision forbids the sending of alcohol for sale in the small or large market under penalty of a fine, and any white can break the container in pieces. Directors and overseers of plantations who catch blacks on their plantations selling alcohol are permitted to punish them. And to prevent fraud and theft, owners of plantations and their overseers are obliged on Sundays and other days when slaves come to market to provide them with a written ticket, properly dated and signed, under penalty that otherwise any white can take from the slaves the fruit, animals, eggs, cassava plants, bananas, oranges, lemons, pineapples, and so on that they have with them. Whites and free blacks who buy from slaves who have no such authorization are subject to a fine. A *placaat* of 1775, to prevent the theft of cotton, forbids the private planting or selling of cotton by slaves.[38] Sellers of cotton, sugar, alcohol, or coffee are obliged to bring their produce to market themselves, or send it with a white person with appropriate authorization. Penalties are established for free blacks as well as whites who buy these products otherwise. For St. Eustatius, a similar *placaat* of 1790 prohibits the selling of poultry and other animals by slaves without a ticket, again with express mention of the problem of theft.[39] A *placaat* of 9 August 1796 (which seems not to have survived) extended the prohibition to wooden boards, planks, and ironwork, and both *placaaten* were extended to furniture, gold and silver work and other items in 1798.[40]

In Surinam, in contrast, the restrictions that might be placed in this group seem primarily aimed at curbing fraud by slaveowners. Thus, in 1757, expressly because of the abuse of hiring out a slave successively to two lessees for the same time and then making excuses for nonperformance, a *placaat* ordered such successive hirings to be reported within fourteen days to the secretary of the colony, subject to penalties.[41] Similar attempts to restrain frauds by owners are in *placaaten* forbidding the selling[42] or pledging[43] of slaves who have not been paid for. A very different explanation lies for the *placaat* of 1767 forbidding owners hiring out slaves in Paramaribo under any pretext whatever, except for public lands or to the company.[44] There were more slaves than were thought to be needed, and if keeping slaves was unproductive, their numbers would be reduced.[45]

From this second group of *placaaten* one might be tempted to deduce that attitudes toward slaves were much harsher in Curaçao than in Surinam. But the contrary is true. It is a commonplace that slaves were much better treated and that the distinction between slave and free was much less marked in Curaçao than it was in Surinam.[46] Law is a distorting mirror. It is, I suggest, precisely because slaves were in practice much less restricted in Curaçao than in Surinam that *placaaten* were more wanted in the former to restrain them.[47] In this chapter as in the rest of the book my concern is with the law, and, as far as possible, I refrain from discussing economic and social conditions. In this context it is enough to note that economic conditions were vastly different in Curaçao and Surinam, yet the differences are scarcely noticeable in the *placaaten*.

A further grouping might be made of those *placaaten* which provided regulations for slaves and free blacks together or which concerned free blacks alone. Thus, for Curaçao, a *placaat* of 1710 forbade Negroes and mulattoes to be on the street after the tattoo without a letter from their master.[48] Likewise, a *placaat* of 1737 forbade them from throwing stones.[49] Another of 1741 forbade assemblies of blacks and mulattoes, and specifically ordered that at burials there should be present no more than six persons.[50] Blacks and mulattoes were also forbidden to carry sticks or cudgels;[51] and attempts were made to restrain their wantonness, especially in singing insulting songs,[52] and to prevent them from throwing rubbish and filth in certain areas of the town.[53] Free blacks and mulattoes also had to enroll themselves for taxation[54] and take part in the night watch.[55]

Surinam does not provide such a rich collection of regulations for slaves and free blacks, but there was a prohibition against drink being sold to them.[56] There was a prohibition against white women living together with Negroes.[57] In 1782 it was provided that, in selling slaves, mothers were not to be separated from their children.[58] And free Negroes and mulattoes had to serve in the watch.[59]

Both in Curaçao[60] and in Surinam general regulations were issued for the behavior of blacks. These in general repeat *placaaten* that I have already discussed. That of Curaçao of 24–28 July 1750 provided in Section 1 that no slaves, whether mulattoes or Negroes, were to congregate with one another in Willemstad, outside the Steenpadspoort, on the other side of the harbor, or elsewhere by day or by night for any assembly or meeting. Much less were they to play on drums, fiddles, or other instruments, or dance or hang out flags, on pain of immediate arrest and severe punishment. By section 2 no slave burial was to be attended by more than six Negroes or mulattoes, and they had to return home immediately afterward. By section 3 no Negroes or mulattoes were to walk the street after 9 P.M. unless they had been provided with a ticket from their owner. Section 4 prohibited whites, free blacks and mulattoes, and slaves from drawing beer in front of slaves or raising jollity or hanging out flags. Section 5 forbade slaves to fight with one another with fists, sticks, knives, or other weapons. And section 7 forbade whites, free Negroes, and mulattoes giving or selling weapons to slaves.[61]

There were also provisions in Curaçao[62] and St. Maarten[63] to prevent whites mishandling free blacks or slaves who were not their own. And for Curaçao there were general regulations for the treatment of slaves by their owners, for example restricting work by slaves on Sundays and feast days and regulating their work hours, food, and clothing.[64] By article 6 owners were forbidden to punish slaves intemperately or unreasonably or for the misdeed of another.

I have given this account of the contents of the *placaaten* of the American colonies of the Dutch West India Company at considerable length because it is important to appreciate their significance, and it is easy to mischaracterize the law. Apart from a few *placaaten* from Surinam still to be looked at on manumission, we have considered all the principal categories of rules set out in the Dutch primary legal sources. They give a very misleading picture compared with slave law in the rest of America. The problem is that the sources are not directly comparable to the sources from elsewhere. The problem is the fact that the rules of Roman law applied, as they were set out in the *Corpus Juris Civilis* and as understood by later scholars, was so taken for granted that they were not restated. And little of this law was changed. The *placaaten* basically added only local police law. And since this is set forth in governors' ordinances, it achieves undue significance in Dutch America. In contrast, for the French colonies, for example, there is the *Code noir*, and for Spanish America the *Real Cédula* of 31 May 1789, both of which set out an account of the law as a whole: the basic private law is given its full weight. For Portuguese America, though there was no official state-ment of the whole law, the secondary work of Perdigão Malheiro, *A Escravidão no Brasil*, allows us to see law in the round. Rome itself, above all, presents a misleading contrast. The law set out in the *Corpus Juris* does not give many of the policing regulations, for behavior in the streets, or for the organization of the markets, but we can be sure they existed. Just as we know—but not from legal sources—that in the later republic the assemblies passed much legis-lation on transitory or political matters[65]—so we can be certain that the curule aediles in charge of streets and markets produced regulations to control who could trade and in what things in order to restrict traffic in stolen goods, and so on. These laws would be too minor, too local, or too subject to change to merit the attention of jurists, and they did not find their way into the *Corpus Juris*.[66] I have already mentioned that the *placaaten* of the Dutch West India Company have an emphatic public law dimension akin to the legis-lation in English America, but it should now be stressed that their substance is much closer to the public law rules promulgated for Spanish America. A few other Spanish examples selected from E. Bentura Beleña, *Autos Acordados* (1787), will make this even clearer. Thus, an *ordenanza* of 17 June 1583 forbade any Indian, black, or mulatto, whether male or female, slave or free, to carry a pointed butcher's knife.[67] An *ordenanza* and *auto acordado* of 2 April 1612 forbade more than three blacks to come together in a public or concealed place by day or by night under a claim of a confraternity or any other reason.[68] An *ordenanza* and *auto acor-dado* of 14 April 1612 forbade more than four blacks, male or female, to gather together at the burial of a black or mulatto, free or slave.[69] It also among other provisions forbade black or mulatto women, free or slave, to wear jewelry of gold, silver, pearls, or *vestidos de Castilla* or silk mantles or trimmings of gold or silver.[70] The really significant contrast with English America is, of course, the absence from Spanish and Dutch America (as from ancient Rome) of such restrictive legislative provisions as those forbidding owners to teach slaves to read or write, compelling owners to inflict

fixed penalties on recaptured runaways, and imposing serious restrictions on manumission.

What the *placaaten* we have so far looked at concern are precisely
those parts of the law which are not dealt with in the *Corpus Juris*.
And the law of slavery other than in the *placaaten* was the pure law
of the *Corpus Juris*. There had been no subsequent continuing development in the United Provinces as there had been in Spain and no
comprehensive legislation as for the French colonies.

Accordingly, although it is nowhere so stated, slaves in the Dutch
West India Company colonies, just as slaves at Rome, had no legal
personality. What is significant, of course, is that no *placaat* directly
addresses the issue, and no *placaat* indirectly indicates that slaves
had legal personality. Likewise, again never directly raised and nowhere indirectly indicated, a slave, like a Roman slave, could not be
married, whether to another slave or a free person. Acquisitions by
a master through slaves and the law relating to contracts made by a
slave would be governed by Roman law, except for the minor modifications already noticed. I noted in passing that slaves could have a
peculium, and the law of the *peculium* would then be as that of
Rome. The private law relating to injuries to or by a slave would be
(or in the absence of evidence about noxal surrender perhaps should
be) that of Rome. The master's right to punish a slave, as set out in
the *placaat* of 20–24 November 1795 for Curaçao, is the same as
that set out in the *Corpus Juris* for the time of Justinian.

One odd issue should be mentioned. At Rome, a slave who was
properly manumitted by a Roman citizen became a Roman citizen.
But what was the legal status of slaves freed by Dutch citizens?
There is no answer in standard legal logical terms. Slavery was not
accepted in the United Provinces. The colonies were not colonies of
the United Provinces but of a trading company, and there was no
citizenship in such a colony. Slaves could be owned by Dutch citizens in the colonies, and their ownership there was recognized by
the courts of the United Provinces. But in these circumstances it is
not easy to provide any convincing argument that a manumitted
slave did or did not become a Dutch citizen. The most that can be

said, in the absence of direct treatment in the sources, primary or secondary, is that there is no evidence that Dutch citizenship was granted to manumitted slaves in the colonies.

Though no changes were made in the law of manumission in other colonies, Surinam did issue regulations. The earliest and basic *placaat* dates from 28 July 1733.[71] The changes from Roman law are modest. Basically, the owner's right to manumit without hindrance remained. Article 1 did require that an owner wishing to manumit by will or *inter vivos* obtain permission from the Edele Hove van Politie, but this is expressly to ensure that the freed person could maintain himself and not be a burden on the finances of the colony. Roman law also showed concern that a freed slave not be a burden on the society. The requirement in article 2 that the freed person show respect to the patron, his wife, children, and descendants corresponds to Roman law.[72] So does reenslavement in article 3 for wronging the patron or his wife.[73] The requirement in article 4 that the person seeking to free a slave bind himself to instruct and bring the slave up in the Christian religion is new. Article 5 obliging freedmen to support patrons and their descendants who fell into poverty is the same as Roman law.[74] Article 6, that a manumitted slave could enter marriage, but not with an existing slave, is the same as Roman law. Article 7, to the effect that the descendants of freed slaves should inherit from them in accordance with the rules of the aasdoms law of Holland, is in a sense an innovation but one to be expected and therefore unexceptionable. It was more reasonable to have as the law of succession that of Amsterdam than that of ancient Rome. Article 8, which established penalties for freed mulattoes, Indians, or blacks of either sex who procreated children with slaves, is an innovation. Article 9, which provided that a manumitted slave with no children had to leave by will one-quarter of his property to his patron or his children, corresponds in principle to the rules of Roman law (which were often changed).[75]

The contents of this *placaat* were repeated in another of 30 January 1741.[76] Another *placaat* of 4 February 1761[77] is to much the same effect. But by article 9 freed persons were not to be found at slaves' festivities: for the second offense the penalty was reenslavement for the benefit of the colony. Article 10 demanded, under penalty, that freed persons show respect to all whites.

Of all the systems of slavery in the Americas, that of the colonies of the Dutch West India Company is perhaps the most instructive for the main thesis of this book, both for the general thesis of the importance of the legal tradition even in very changed geographical, moral, economic, and social conditions and for the particular thesis of the central importance of Roman law in the legal tradition of the Western world. Roman law had been received in the United Provinces. But slavery was not accepted, and therefore neither was the Roman law of slavery. The social institution of slavery was accepted in the colonies of the Dutch West India Company without the authorization of the Dutch States-General. The company, then, neither authorized to take any legal system as governing slavery nor to make a law of its own, simply took over Roman law in its entirety. The obvious explanation for this is the general Reception of Roman law in the United Provinces. Thereafter, this law, in its private law aspects, remained virtually unchanged, even though the law was made on the spot, not in the home country, not by the States-General of the United Provinces but by the governor and council of the individual colony. The only other colonies where law was made on the spot were the English colonies. In England there had been no Reception of Roman law, and Roman law is not prominent in English colonial legislation, which was the major factor in legal development. In the Dutch company's colonies, the basics of Roman law were accepted without question, and not much was altered by gubernatorial intervention.

8

SOME COMPARISONS

It is a phenomenon of the law of slavery that some detail or expression of the law in one system catches the imagination of scholars, who then attribute undue significance to it. Accounts of the law, especially as compared with that of other systems, become very misleading. In this chapter three separate instances of this phenomenon will be discussed: the emphasis in Spanish law that liberty is natural;[1] the distinction frequently drawn between chattel slavery (in English America) and slavery involving almost a contractual relationship (in Latin America); and Somersett's case.

That the Spanish emphasis on liberty is connected with the Roman legal sources has long been known, so it is right to begin with them. Their point has, sadly, been misconstrued.[2] But something more must first be said about the nature of Justinian's *Digest*, *Code*, and *Institutes*. The *Digest* of 533 A.D. is a collection of extracts from classical jurists of centuries before, and, despite the general opinion, Justinian did not give his compilers instructions to change the texts and bring them up to date. On the contrary, they were told (in addition to abridging and cutting out what was obsolete) not to repeat what was declared elsewhere, that is, in the first edition of the *Code* of 529.[3] The *Code* consists of imperial decrees and decisions, mainly from the third century onward. Thus when these works are taken together, the *Digest* is an abridgment of Roman classical law minus what had become obsolete and minus what was repeated by laws in the *Code*; and the *Code* gave the subsequent amendments. The *Code* of 529 was replaced by a revised version in 534 and, as a consequence, it has not survived. There is no relevant text in the *Code* of 534 on slavery and natural law, but there is in the *Digest* and *Institutes*. The *Institutes* (also of 533) are the short elementary textbook, hence if they contain statements not in the *Digest*, the assumption must be that these statements were not in the writings of the classical jurists. Thus to establish Roman—as distinct from Justinianic—attitudes, we must start with the *Digest*. And though Roman philosophers such as Cicero were interested in the nature of natural law[4] we should not use their works—at least not in the first instance—to establish the attitude of the lawyers. The jurists' purpose was different. The sole relevant *Digest* texts are the following:

> D.1.1.1.3 (Ulpian, Institutes, book 1). *Ius naturale*, natural law is that which nature has taught all animals. For it is law not specific to humankind, but of all animals which are born on land and in the sea. It is also shared by the birds. Hence comes the union of male and female which we call marriage, and the procreation and rearing of children. For we see that the other animals too, even wild beasts, are credited with knowledge of that law. 4. *Ius gentium*, the law of nations, is that which human nations use. That it is not coextensive with natural law is easily understood, because the latter is common to all animals, the former only to human beings among themselves.[5]
>
> D.1.5.4. (Florentinus, Institutes, book 9). Freedom is the natural power of doing what one pleases, except what is prohibited by force or law. 1. Slavery is an institution of the *ius gentium*, by which a person contrary to nature is subjected to another's ownership. 2. Slaves [*servi*] are so called because generals have the habit of selling their captives and in this way save [*servare*], not kill, them.[6]

The first point to observe here is that no practical conclusions are drawn from the observation that slavery is contrary to nature. Slavery is not prohibited. On the contrary, it is said to be practiced by all peoples. Second, D.1.1.1.3 and 4 are not intended to give a moral content to *ius naturale*. On the contrary, the distinction is purely factual: *ius naturale* is the law that applies to all animals, whereas *ius gentium* is restricted to humans and is the law accepted by all peoples. Third, and this is a point that seems to have been overlooked, if natural law applies equally to all animals, including humans and wild beasts, and slavery is contrary to it, then so should be the keeping in captivity of animals such as cattle or sheep. One might deduce one of two propositions from this. One can suggest that the jurists had not noticed this conclusion, and the proposition would then indicate that the jurists were little interested in the issue of natural law.[7] Or one can suggest that the jurists were aware that the keeping of animals was contrary to natural law (in their sense), but the point was not made because it was unimportant, and in *D.*1.5.4 the issue arose only because the jurists wanted to distinguish between the status of freedom and slavery. On this latter approach, the proposition would again illustrate that there was no moral dimension to the notion of natural law. Fourth, the stress in *D.*1.5.4. is on liberty being the natural state, and it is only in contrast to that that slavery cannot be natural. There is the implication that once natural, always natural.

The conclusion that I want to draw from the foregoing is, of course, that when the Roman jurists in the *Digest* say that slavery is contrary to nature, there is no implication that they regard it in any way as improper or blameworthy. Their statements have no moral implications.

Justinian's *Institutes* repeat these texts with a few variations,[8] but also contain a further text: "*J.*1.2.11. But natural law which is observed everywhere and among all peoples is established by a kind of divine providence and remains always stable and immutable. But that law which each state established for itself is often changed either by the tacit approval of the people or by another statute which is subsequently passed."[9] There is no parallel for this in the *Digest* or *Code*, no agreement is found among scholars on a possible source for it,[10] and it is reasonable to think that it must be Justinianic. It sets out an idea that seems already inherent in *D.*1.5.4.1, that natural law is immutable: once natural (like liberty), always natural. But the description of natural law contained in the first sentence of the translation seems more appropriate to the jurists' conception of *ius gentium*, probably the result of insufficient interest in the whole notion. The text, however, does bring in a new dimension: natural law is connected with religion; it is established by a kind of divine providence.[11]

To come now to the celebrated declarations of Spanish law. *Las Siete Partidas* 4.22, at the beginning of the prologue, declares: "By nature all the creatures of the world love and covet liberty. How much more do men who have understanding above all the others, and especially those who have a noble heart."[12] And 4.21.1.: "Slavery is a condition and institution which nations made in ancient times, by which men who were naturally free became slaves. They were subjected to the ownership of others contrary to the reason of nature. The slave [*siervo*] took this name from a word that they call in Latin *servare*, which is as much as to say in Spanish, to save. And this saving was established by the emperors. For in ancient times, as many as they captured, they killed."[13] The dependence of these texts on the Roman ones is readily apparent. By the time of Alfonso the Wise, of course, theologians had much developed the notion of natural law, but again it would be methodologically wrong to assume that the theological notion explains the meaning and intention of the legislator rather than his Roman models.

To take the texts as they stand, again, there is no indication that the institution of slavery is morally wrong. Liberty is natural, but this is true for all animals as well as for humans, as we are expressly told. It follows that if slavery is morally wrong, then so is the captivity and domestication of animals. The emphasis is on liberty as the original, therefore natural, status. I have suggested elsewhere that the derivation of the word *servus*, slave, from *servare*, to save, in the Roman texts might indicate some uneasiness over the morality of slavery.[14] Even if that is so, the text of the *Partidas* seems to be no more than an explanation of the existence of slavery.

The same approach is needed for the preface of *Las Siete Partidas* 4.5, which begins: "Slavery is the lowest and most despised thing that can exist between men. Because man, who is the most noble and free creature, among all the other creatures, that God made, is placed by it in the power of another: in such a way that they can do with him whatever they want, as they can with their other property alive or dead."[15] In this (and in the rest of the preface that has not been quoted) slavery is not condemned as immoral. The legislator is making what is for him a statement of fact: slavery is the most wretched condition of man.

But we must place these texts in the context of the lawmakers' general understanding of natural law. *Las Siete Partidas* 1.1.2 declares:

> *Ius naturale* in Latin means in Spanish *derecho natural* (natural law) which all men have in them naturally, and even the other animals which have feeling. Following the direction of this law, the male unites with the female, which we call marriage; and on this account, humans care for their children; and so do all animals. Furthermore there is *ius gentium* (in Latin), which means the law common to all nations, and not to the other animals. And this was created with reason and also from necessity, because men could not well live with one another in harmony, and in peace if all did not use this law.[16]

Later in the same law Alfonso declares that by the *ius gentium* all men are bound to love God and to obey their parents and their native land. Thus in the main law discussing natural law, no moral content is given to it. That is reserved, if at all, to *ius gentium*.

Those modern scholars who attribute an awareness of the immorality of slavery to the Spanish lawmakers are being anachronistic. But their opinion should not be surprising. From a modern standpoint, after centuries in which the doctrine of natural law has held a central place in theological debate, it is not easy to approach the early legal sources on their own terms. A detail in the standard gloss to *Las Siete Partidas*, which was written in the sixteenth century by Gregorio López, who was a member of the Consejo Real de Indias, is revealing for Spanish legal attitudes in his time. In his gloss on the general treatment of natural law in *Las Siete Partidas* at 1.1.1, he says among other things: "But following the nature which man has in common with angels, that is the power of reasoning, it is thus defined: 'Natural law is a certain reason of nature implanted in the human creature to do good and to avoid the opposite.'" Thus, in this context, for López natural law has a moral quality. And he proceeds to develop this definition following and citing Thomas Aquinas. But when he glosses the laws on slavery there is no indication that he regards the institution as immoral, even though in his gloss on *Las Siete Partidas* 4.21.1 he says it is contrary to nature.

The second topic to which too much significance is attributed is a distinction frequently made by scholars writing on slavery in the Americas between chattel slavery in which the slave is legally a thing, "only the object of rights and never the subject of them," and systems in which the slave is a *legal person* held to bondage for life, who has various obligations on his part as opposed to the condition of the privilege on the part of others."[17] The distinction is fundamental, for example, to the work of Herbert S. Klein, *Slavery in the Americas*, who firmly places slavery in Virginia in the first category, slavery in Cuba in the second.

Whatever value the distinction may have in theory or in other historical contexts,[18] I do not find it illuminating for slavery in the Americas or for its historical antecedents.

A number of issues should be the focus of attention: the capacity of a slave in private law actions, as party or as witness; the slave as defendant or witness in criminal trials; the extent of control over any such fund as the *peculium*; legal recognition of slave families, not just husband and wife but parental rights and duties; obligations of the owner to provide for his slaves; restrictions on the owner's right to punish; and the attitude of the law to attacks on slaves by persons other than the owner. It should be stressed once again at the outset that to recognize that a slave is a human being and has human characteristics (above all, in being capable of forming intentions) is not necessarily to treat the slave in law as anything other than a thing.

If we accept the distinction as meaningful, we must believe that English America had a system of chattel slavery. The issue is really whether one can draw a significant contrast with Latin America.

Again, one must return to Roman law, where, I think, slavery must be classified as chattel slavery. Slaves had no legal personality. They could not marry. They could own nothing; they could use the *peculium* only as allowed by their owner. They could not be a party to a civil lawsuit and could be witnesses only in exceptional circumstances and only under torture. Their redress if they were cruelly treated was not to bring a lawsuit against the owner but to flee to a temple or statue of the emperor, and a judicial inquiry would be held. They had no right to bring an action against the owner to force him to free them even if he had agreed to do so, except when the owner had accepted a price from an outside source. Even then the redress was not a process of the usual type. They could, however, become free automatically as a consequence of an arrangement between their present owner and the transferor of title to him: whether the transferor by his last will gave the slave to the now owner with the command to free him under conditions which have occurred, or whether he was sold to the owner under similar conditions. Still, even Roman law allowed them to intervene as parties in a private law matter in very limited circumstances. That they were human beings was (as in English America) recognized.

Spanish law, and Spanish law in America, took over the basics of Roman law, with modifications. The real issue for us is whether the modifications were sufficient to turn chattel slavery into something else.[19] Slaves basically still had no legal personality and could neither sue nor be sued. Slave marriage was legally recognized, but it had few legal consequences. A slave could bring an action against a cruel master for remedies identical to those in Roman law when a slave fled to a temple or statue of the emperor. There is no practical difference here from Roman law, though there is a theoretical divide. More significant is *coartación*. A slave could bring actions both to have a fair price set on him and to demand his freedom when he paid that price. The development from Roman law and the use of the *peculium* is easily traced, and the practical difference may not have been at all great. Few slaves would have been able to make use of *coartación*, and it is reasonable to suppose that in Rome most of such slaves would have been freed without that development. The difference in theory (and in practice, too) between the Roman law of chattel slavery and the Spanish American law is, I suggest, one of degree and not of kind.[20] No sharp contrast should therefore be made with the law of English America.

(It may be noted that slaves who are in a position to buy freedom will always be those who were already favored by their owner. Of necessity they will be those who were allowed to exercise their talents. However good a surveyor or financier a slave might have been, he will have success only if the owner provided opportunities denied to most slaves. Readers who have worked as wage slaves in a menial capacity will recognize how difficult it is for a boss to accept that they can do anything differently, but better. The standard attitude is that the only way menial workers can work better is for them to work harder. Thus, when slaves buy their freedom there will have been something particular in their earlier relationship with the owner.)

The third detail in slave law that has captured the imagination of some scholars concerns Somersett's case of 1772 in England,[21] which is rightly regarded as a great step forward in promoting liberty but is also seen as a tribute to the efficacy of the writ of habeas corpus and thus of the common law. We need not consider the state of law in England before,[22] nor the precise scope of the decision of Lord Mansfield.[23] It is enough to note that the case came to have a rhetorical value for reformers and scholars which would justify the earlier words of Sir William Blackstone: "And this spirit of liberty is so deeply implanted in our constitution, and rooted even in our very soil, that a slave or a negro, the moment he lands in England, falls under the protection of the laws, and with regard to all natural rights becomes *eo instanti* a freeman."[24] The case was destined to have a great future. One of the counsel for James Somersett, Francis Hargrave, was to make his reputation from a book he published in London also in 1772, entitled *An argument in the case of James Somersett a Negro, lately determined by the Court of King's Bench.*[25] This was republished in Boston in 1774 and again in London in 1775. The work is in the form of a speech on behalf of Somersett though the author declares it was never delivered as such. The learning in it is remarkable, and Hargrave notes instances on the continent of Europe by courts and scholars alike to the effect that a slave brought within their jurisdiction automatically becomes free. The neglect of these instances by subsequent writers is what is so astonishing.[26] Thus for the Netherlands, Hargrave[27] quotes Simon à Groenewegen (1613–52): "Slavery gradually fell from use, and the very name with us today is obsolete; to such an extent, indeed, that slaves who are brought here from elsewhere can proclaim their liberty, even against the wishes of their owner, as soon as they enter the borders of our control. This is accepted by the customs of other Christian peoples."[28]

Groenewegen cites much authority for Holland, Belgium, and elsewhere.[29] Hargrave also refers rightly to Johannes Voet (1647–1713)[30] and J. G. Heineccius's (1681–1741) edition of Arnaldus Vinnius,[31] who were following Groenewegen. For France he refers[32] for the same point to Jean Bodin, *Les six livres de la république*, 1.5 (first published in 1579). For English-speaking readers this citation should have been even more à propos because the work appeared in an English translation in 1606. The appropriate passage reads:

> But in Fraunce, although there be some remembrance of old servitude, yet is it not lawful there to make any slave, or to buy any of others: Inso much that the slaves of strangers so soone as they set their foot within Fraunce become franke & free; as was by an old decree of the court of Paris determined against an ambassador of Spain, who had brought a slave with him into Fraunce. And I remember that of late a Genua marchant having brought with him into Tholouze a slave whome he had bought in Spaine, the hoast of the house understanding the matter, persuaded the slave to appeale unto his libertie. The matter being brought before the magistrats, the marchant was called for; the Atturney general out of the records showed certaine auntient priveledges given (as is said) unto them of Tholouze by Theodosius the Great, wherein he had granted, That slaves so soone as they came into Tholouze should be free. The marchant alledging for himselfe that he had truly bought his slave in Spain, and so was afterward come to Tholouze, from thence to goe home to Genua, and so not to be bound to the laws of Fraunce. In the end hee requested that if they would needs deale so hardly with him, as to set at libertie another mans slave, yet they should at least restore unto him the money hee cost him: whereunto the Iudges aunswered, That it was a matter to be considered of. In the meane time the marchant fearing least he should loose both his dutifull slave and his money also of himselfe set him at libertie, yet covenanting with him that he should serve him so long as he lived. Yet for all that, those priveledges which they of Tholouze boast to have bene granted them by Theodosius, seeme not to have bene so, seeing that Narbona a true Colonie of the Romans, and the most auntient that was in Fraunce, Lectore, Nismes, Vienne, Lyons, Arles, Ro-

mans, and many others, which were also Roman Collonies, no nor
Rome it selfe the verie seat of the Empire, had not any such priveledge.
And thus much concerning the enfranchising of slaves.[33]

Charondas, who is also cited by Groenewegen, describes a case of
1538.[34] An Italian brought into France a slave who was Greek by
origin. The Italian then died, and his heirs brought an action claiming the Greek who had entered the service of an "honneste seig-
neur" and this last successfully defended the action. The Greek was
declared free in accordance with the common law of France.

The relevant point in all this for us is not that the importance of
the subsequent role of Somersett's case in Anglo-American law
should be downgraded. Rather, it is that in a country where slavery
is not recognized and slaves from outside are brought within the
territory, any rule that they are treated as free has nothing particular
to do with England, English concepts of freedom, the particular
efficacy of habeas corpus, or the glory of the common law. The same
result was reached without legislation in civil law jurisdictions such
as France, Holland, and Belgium much earlier.[35] By a Portuguese
constitution of 19 September 1761, slaves transmitted from Brazil
to Portugal became free.[36] For Holland, as we have seen in chapter
7, the ruling was modified by 1736 so that only slaves from other
than Dutch possessions became free on reaching Holland.[37] (But
Hargrave should not be faulted for not saying so because the relevant ruling was not published until later).

The three details or expressions of law discussed in this chapter
also indicate something of the significance of comparative law. The
meaning of natural law in *Las Siete Partidas* is most clearly uncovered when we also look at the Roman texts. The limited contrast
between English America and Latin America with regard to chattel
slavery comes to light only when we consider the dependence of the
latter's law on Roman law. And claims made for the common law
because of Somersett's case can be properly evaluated only when we
take account of similar developments in continental Europe. At the
lowest estimate, the importance of the appearance of approaches,
details, rules, and structures in a legal system can be estimated only
in conjunction with comparative historical analysis.

9

CONCLUSIONS ON LAW

AND SOCIETY

The preceding chapters on slave law are, I believe, very revealing in many ways, and conclusions can be drawn from them for a number of issues. The conclusions are best set out in two chapters even though this will cause some overlap. This first of these chapters is devoted to conclusions that may be drawn for the general relationship between law and society.

To begin with, the astounding frequency and importance of legal transplants is again illustrated. Roman law was the starting point, hence I have not discussed the extent to which it may have borrowed from any Greek system. My impression, for what it is worth, is that Roman law was relatively free from borrowing. And, though the issue has not been directly addressed, investigation would show that if one accepted English America as a single unit, much of the legislation was original, not borrowed. But English America was composed of numerous colonies (later, states), and these borrowed their legislation from one another. Thus in South Carolina the earliest statute was largely copied from the law of Barbados. And South Carolina's law was borrowed by other colonies. English American judges, however, borrowed from Roman law. Roman law to a great extent was transplanted to Spain, especially in the form of *Las Siete Partidas*, and from there to the New World. France, which had rejected slavery and a law of slavery, gave a new life to Roman law in the French colonies. Law can be resurrected even when it is dead.

The longevity of much of law is also in evidence. The best example, among many, is the survival of many ancient Roman rules in the second half of the nineteenth century in Brazil. The capacity of legal rules to remain in force, sometimes unchanged, sometimes with modification, in very different political, social, and economic circumstances is again emphasized.

The lack of interest on the part of governments in developing private law is highlighted. Governments often either do not legislate or when they do they borrow from elsewhere, with little regard for the changed circumstances of their own country. Thus the Roman state intervened very little to influence the growth of law relating to slaves. Above all, it did not take the initiative in creating the law on manumission. Yet Roman citizenship was a highly prized treasure. The state allowed almost any owner, with almost no restrictions, to free almost any slave, in any numbers, in a way that gave them citizenship. Since in the early Roman Empire citizens received a ration of free food and entrance to the games, the manumission of slaves by a master was not without economic consequences for the rest of society.[1] The Spanish rulers, especially King Alfonso X in *Las Siete Partidas*, did legislate, but they took over Roman law to such an extent that one must believe they had no particular views of their own on what the appropriate law ought to be. They exported this slave law to their American colonies, where conditions of servitude were very different. Despite the very different character of New World slavery, changes in the law were slow in coming. The extent to which France, too, borrowed from Roman law is significant in a different way. France had no slaves, so none of its system of law (even in the guise of the *Coutume de Paris*) could provide a law for slavery in the French colonies. Legislation was accordingly prepared, with Roman law as the model, and a modified nonracist slave law was imposed on a racist slave society. Again, one must feel that the French king and his lawmakers were more interested simply in having legal rules than in promulgating any particular political, social, or economic message in the rules.[2] Neither Portugal nor subsequently Brazil seemed to have much interest in substituting homemade rules for Roman rules made for a very different society. The same holds true for the colonies of the Dutch West India Company. English America was different. In this case there was much legislation, but in English America slavery was given a public dimension that was lacking in the other societies, particularly Rome, that we have looked at.

Some other aspects of the relationship between law and society also become clearer. Rome was a slaveowning society, where slavery was not based on race, and racism does not appear in the law. English America was a very racist society, and this is very much reflected in the law. And the law of slavery in English America was largely made without a preceding model. In contrast, Spanish, Portuguese, Dutch, and French America all had slavery based on racism but had a law of slavery that was not so overtly racist as that of English America. The explanation in the case of Portuguese America is the direct use of Roman law to fill the (very numerous) gaps in the law; and in the case of Spanish America in the indirect influence of Roman slave law, mediated through the slave law adopted in Castile. Little more was done in Dutch America than to add something of a public law dimension to the private Roman law of slavery (which itself had simply been accepted as law in the colonies without a firm legal foundation).

French America is particularly revealing for the importance of a purely legal tradition for the development of legal rules. France was faced with the issue of framing a law of slavery for its American colonies. It had no slave law of its own, nor was Roman law entrenched in the jurisdictions of France as the one system to make use of in developing the law. It shared that role with *coutumes* of other regions in general and with the *Coutume de Paris* in particular. Its role varied from one jurisdiction to another. Yet when a law of slavery was needed and *coutumes* provided no guidance, the legislators took Roman law as their model. The differences between slavery as it existed in society in Rome and in French America played a lesser role in the promulgation of the *Code noir*. Thus, Roman law, received in four different ways in Spain, Portugal, the United Provinces, and France, had a dominant influence on the law of slavery in their respective colonies.

In such circumstances it would be presumptuous to believe that if Roman law had been received in England, Roman slave law would *not* have had a very powerful effect on the law of slavery in the English colonies and southern states. (As it was, Roman law influenced the judges). A consequence would have been that the slave law in English America would have been far less racist.

But law is also influenced by social, economic, and political factors, if only slowly at times. Thus for Spanish America, especially for Santo Domingo, the law became more overtly racist, and this happened even earlier in French Louisiana. Yet something more seems to be involved. Racism was expressed in law in Spanish and French America by making manumission more difficult, by allowing masters to punish more, by making it more difficult to give financial support to free blacks, and by treating free blacks as being closer to slaves; and it became harsher by allowing masters to punish more severely. But English American slave law was racist from the start, and yet, with the passage of time, it too became harsher to slaves and free blacks in exactly the same way. Just to say that the society became more racist seems unsatisfactory. In contrast, something very different happened in ancient Rome. Manumission became ever less formal, and the master's rights to punish became more restricted.

The simplest explanation is that the Roman state came ever more to trust that owners would free the "right slaves," whereas the legislatures for the Americas came to distrust owners freeing slaves, who would remain in the colony or state.[3] Yet in all these societies the slaves who would be freed would be similar (except that in Rome and some parts of Spanish America a slave might have considerable earning power and be freed in consequence); they would be those close to the master through service or a sexual or blood relationship. Such bonds were acceptable in Rome, but not in the Americas, again because of racism. With regard to the law on punishing slaves, the Roman state did not trust owners not to ill-treat their slaves: their other slaves, of course. In English America especially, fixed penalties to be inflicted on slaves by the owner had to be laid down simply because the state did not trust the owner to punish some slaves to the extent that the legislature considered sufficient.

A conclusion that is implicit through much of the book ought perhaps to be made express. When a foreign legal system is treated by other societies as a resource for borrowing from, the borrowing may occur in multifarious ways. This is especially pronounced with regard to slave law because not all the colonial powers of Europe which accepted slavery in the colonies had retained it at home. Thus Spain received Roman law and recognized the social institution of slavery. It produced much law of its own on slavery, very heavily influenced by Roman law. This Romanized law was transplanted to America, but Roman law was not directly applicable there. Portugal also received Roman law and recognized slavery. It produced its own legislation, which was incomplete in many respects, and Roman law remained directly applicable as subsidiary law. This system was transplanted to Portuguese America, where slavery and Roman slave law were given renewed vigor. France underwent a Reception of Roman law but did not recognize slavery, hence did not receive Roman slave law. For its colonies France promulgated codes of slave law which were strongly influenced by Roman law. But Roman law was not directly applicable in French America. The Dutch United Provinces received Roman law but not slavery. Apparently by ingenious misinterpretation, the Dutch West India Company accepted Roman law as regulating slavery and left it largely unchanged. It was not so much subsidiary law as it was the primary law. England did not undergo a Reception, but English American judges adopted the habit of using Roman law to fill gaps in the law relating to slaves. One incidental result of this approach to law and lawmaking in the Americas is that, in the various territories, different aspects of the substantive law appear to be stressed, without the apparent difference in emphasis having much always to do with real differences in the law.

A further conclusion is to very different effect. The analysis shows how difficult it is to deduce much about a society from an examination of its legal rules.

10

CONCLUSIONS ON SLAVERY
AND SLAVE LAW

On the basis of the foregoing chapters it is also possible, I believe, to draw some conclusions on slavery and slave law. These can be set out in the form of propositions in three groups, A, B, and C.

A.

1. In a slaveholding society in which slavery is not based on race, manumission and the grant of citizenship may (depending on all other circumstances) be given relatively easily. The government, indeed, may show little interest in the subject, allowing owners great freedom to manumit slaves.

2. Also, in a society in which slavery is not based on race, there is no objection, on the basis of the slave's supposed lack of intelligence, to masters training slaves. (There may, at times, be other objections, such as fear of competition in the labor market with free persons.)

3. In contrast, in a society in which slavery is based on race, one would expect obstacles to be placed in the way of owners freeing slaves and of the incorporation of any freed slave into the society. Indeed, when we find racist societies some of which have extensive legal obstacles to manumission, others many fewer obstacles, it is the absence of legal obstacles that has to be explained.

4. In a racist slaveowning society one would expect restrictions to be placed on the education or training of slaves and on the type of work they can do. Their inferiority, including supposed intellectual inferiority, will thereby be stressed.

5. In a racist slave society there is likely to be emphasis on a public dimension to slavery that may be less obvious in a nonracist slave society. That already appears from proposition 4, but it is likely also to extend to owners being legally obliged to punish slaves for certain behavior, to other members of the society having the right to question slaves' behavior, and to slaves being required to show "respect" to all members of the ruling race. In this regard freed slaves and their descendants are likely to be placed somewhat in the position of slaves.

6. Even in the nonracist slave society certain categories of slaves are much more likely to be freed than others: the owner's mistress, his children (or parents), wet nurse, teacher, and loyal servant, or slaves who by their efforts have put themselves in the position of being able to "buy" their freedom. In a very racist society some owners will still want to free some slaves, who will have similar characteristics to those most often manumitted in a nonracist slave society. It is no contradiction that even a very racist slaveowner may well want some of *his* slaves to be free.

7. Manumission of slaves is frequently accompanied by monetary gifts or financial support, especially because of the relationship of friendship, respect, or blood that exists between the freed person and his patron.

8. Incorporation into the society of freed slaves and their descendants is easier if they have funds. This is especially so where slavery is racist (since in nonracist slave societies, the freed slaves and their descendants blend in with the rest of the population). This makes proposition 7 significant. "Money makes white."[1]

9. Where manumission is prohibited or is very restricted, some owners will still try to free some slaves, especially by making use of a device such as a trust. Some such attempts will succeed, some will fail. But inevitably the supply of freed persons will be smaller than it otherwise would be, both because of the restrictions themselves and because the descendants of slaves in de facto freedom are likely to fall back into real slavery when the trust ends or is attacked or neglected.

10. Where manumission is prohibited or restricted, there are

likely also to be prohibitions on routing funds to former slaves or setting up trusts for the financial benefit of slaves. This is especially significant because of proposition 8.

11. The corollary of propositions 9 and 10 is that when there are no or few restrictions on manumission or gifts there will be more and wealthier freed persons and their descendants than would otherwise be the case.

B.

12. Because of the wide range and large number of influencing factors it is not possible to estimate how, if the law in force were the same, the proportion of manumissions would vary from one society to another.

13. Likewise and for similar reasons it is not possible to estimate in one racist society or another the effect of different sizes of populations of slave descendants, many of whom are materially comfortable.

14. But one can hold on to the legal rules as something solid, and above all one can make something out of propositions 9, 10, and 11.

15. And one can reasonably hold that there has to be some impact on racist societies of population of varying size of "free blacks" who are moderately well off.

C.

16. The development of law is strongly affected by the legal tradition.

17. Ancient Rome was a slaveowning society where slavery was not based on race. The law relating to slaves reflects this. Slaveholding was strictly a matter between owner and slave. There were no restrictions on the training or employment of slaves. Manumission by the owner was relatively unrestricted, and there was no restriction on providing freed slaves with property.

18. The parts of English America which were slave societies had racist slavery. This is powerfully demonstrated in the law that developed. Slave law had a strong public dimension. Masters might not educate their slaves as they wished, they were legally obliged in some states to punish them in certain ways for particular behavior, and stringent restrictions were placed on manumission and on providing funds for slaves or former slaves.

19. The American colonies of France, Spain, Portugal, and the Dutch West Indian Company and the states that developed from them had slavery based on race. But each colony received a system of a law of slavery based on Roman law.

20. Insofar as the slave law in Latin and Dutch America remained unchanged or developed on the basis of its European tradition, the law remained nonracist in its rules.

21. Insofar as this law was unchanged, insofar as manumission was subject to few restrictions and so was more frequent than would otherwise have been the case, insofar as favorable financial circumstances enabled descendants of slaves to be more acceptable, then the differences (which have often been remarked on) between English America on one hand and Latin and Dutch America on the other, especially with regard to the frequency of manumission and the treatment of descendants of slaves, can be explained sufficiently (though, of course, not completely) by the impact of the legal tradition.

22. The legal rules, then, are no guide for determining whether English America was more racist than Latin or Dutch America.

23. Law for the Latin American colonies was primarily made by the European power. Lawmakers in the colonies were in favor of more racist law.

24. Law in Dutch and English America was made on the spot in the colony or state. But the Dutch, unlike the English, had accepted Roman law as the basis of the legal regime of slavery, and the law always continued to allow manumission easily. Even where law is made in a society that has a racist social system of slavery, slave law inherited from Rome will continue to show important elements of the nonracist Roman slave law.

NOTES

1. An exception is Louisiana, which is dealt with only when it was first in the hands of the French. Its subsequent history under Spain, again under France, and then as part of the United States (involving questions of whether the law in use was basically French- or Spanish-inspired) is ignored.

2. An instructive example is furnished by the essays collected by Laura Foner and Eugene D. Genovese, *Slavery in the New World* (Englewood Cliffs, N.J., 1969). Many of the articles discuss arguments drawn from law, but the authors are historians, sociologists, and anthropologists. Not one is a lawyer, legal historian, or comparative legal historian. A very different thesis, to explain differences in the extent of racism in the Americas, in which differences in law scarcely appear, is H. Hoetink, *The Two Variants in Caribbean Race Relations* (London, 1967); and Hoetink, *Slavery and Race Relations in the Americas* (New York, 1973).

3. (New York, 1946).

4. I am persuaded by the arguments of J. P. Tardieu, *Le destin des noirs aux Indes de Castille, XVIᵉ–XVIIIᵉ siècles* (Paris, 1984), that the differences between Spanish America and English America were not so great (passim, but see esp. pp. 314ff.).

5. Stanley Elkins, *Slavery, a Problem in American Institutional and Intellectual Life*, 2d ed. (1959; rpt. Chicago, 1968), pp. 250f.

6. Ibid., pp. 245ff.

7. But for ambiguity inherent in the attitude of members of Catholic religious orders, see, e.g., Tardieu, *Destin*, pp. 17, 65, 163f., 320ff.; Antoine Gisler, *L'Esclavage aux Antilles Françaises* (Fribourg, 1965), pp. 55ff., 151ff.

8. See Elkins, *Slavery*, pp. 250f.

9. See, Naphtali Lewis, *Life in Egypt under Roman Rule* (Oxford, 1983), pp. 57, 116.

10. *De rebus rusticis* 1.17.3.

11. See, e.g., the Georgia case of *Gorman v. Campbell*, 14 Ga. 137 (1853). For the practice of hiring out slaves see R. B. Campbell, "Slave Hiring in Texas," *American Historical Review* 93 (1988): 167ff.

12. For some illuminating details of the impact of sugar harvesting see the anonymous *Negro Slavery; Or, a View of Some of the More Prominent Features of That State of Society, as It Exists in the United States of America and in the Colonies of the West Indies, Especially in Jamaica*, published with William Wilberforce, *An Appeal to the Religion, Justice, and Humanity of the Inhabitants of the British Empire, in Behalf of the Negro Slaves in the West Indies* (London, 1823), pp. 38ff.; Gisler, *L'Esclavage*, p. 195; William Goodell, *The American Slave Code* (1853; rpt. New York, 1968), pp. 79f., 133f.; G. M. Hall, *Social Control in Slave Plantation Societies* (Baltimore, 1971), pp. 13ff. Just as greed, not sadism or racism, is the main cause of enslavement, so the main cause of systematic ill-treatment is greed, not sadism or racism.

13. But women might have a better survival rate than men; see Nicole Vanony-Frisch, *Les Esclaves de la Guadelupe à la fin de l'Ancien Régime d'après les sources notariales, 1770–1789* (Guadelupe, 1985), pp. 62f.

1. THE GENERAL THESIS

1. For this proposition see Alan Watson, *Failures of the Legal Imagination* (Philadelphia, 1988), pp. 35ff.

2. I use the term *government* as consistently as possible to indicate the individual or group who has, individually or collectively, both the highest executive powers in the state and the right to issue legal commands in the form of statute or a close approximation.

3. See W. W. Buckland, *Textbook of Roman Law*, 3d ed., rev. by Peter Stein (Cambridge, 1963), p. 4; Max Kaser, *Das römische Privatrecht*, 2d ed. (Munich, 1971), 1:181; J. A. C. Thomas, *Textbook of Roman Law* (Amsterdam, 1976), pp. 4f., 40ff.

4. See H. J. Wolff, *Roman Law: An Historical Introduction* (Norman, Okla., 1951), pp. 172ff.; Kaser, *Das römische Privatrecht*, 1:1; Thomas, *Textbook*, pp. 7ff.

5. See Gerald Strauss, *Law, Resistance, and the State* (Princeton, 1986), pp. 73ff.

6. See O. F. Robinson, et al., *Introduction to European Legal History* (Abingdon, 1985), p. 61.

7. See Watson, *Failures*, pp. 145f.

8. See ibid., pp. 47ff.

9. See S. F. C. Milsom, *Historical Foundations of the Common Law*, 2d

ed. (Toronto, 1981), passim; F. Reynold, *The Judge as Lawmaker* (London, 1967), p. 7.

10. See Alan Watson, *Sources of Law, Legal Change, and Ambiguity* (Philadelphia, 1984), pp. 2ff.

11. See Alan Watson, review of Bruce Frier, *The Rise of the Roman Jurists, Michigan Law Review* 85 (1987): 1071ff. at pp. 1075f.

12. See Watson, *Sources of Law*, pp. 9ff.

13. See Alan Paterson, *The Law Lords* (London, 1982), pp. 9ff., esp. pp. 33f.

14. See Fritz Schulz, *Roman Legal Science* (Oxford, 1953), pp. 44f. J. W. Tellegen argues unconvincingly that there was no sharp distinction between orators and jurists: "*Oratores, Jurisprudentes* and the *Causa Curiana*," *Revue Internationale des Droits de l'Antiquité* 30 (1983), pp. 293ff.; "*Parva Quaestio sed tamen Quaestio*," *Juridical Review* 195 (1987): 195ff.

15. *Top.* 12.51.

16. See J. F. Stephen, *History of the Criminal Law of England* (London, 1883), 1:461.

17. Cf. *D*.29.5; *Pauli Sententiae* 3.5.

18. *D*.29.5.1*pr.*

19. *D*.29.5.1.2.

20. *D*.29.5.1.3.

21. *D*.29.5.1.7.

22. *D*.29.5.1.8.

23. *D*.29.5.1.9.

24. *D*.29.5.1.10.

25. See Otto Lenel, *Das Edictum perpetuum*, 3d ed. (Leipzig, 1927), p. 363f. The positioning of the *senatus consultum* in the Edict would be a bureaucratic act but presumably with juristic involvement, and it was obviously approved by Julian.

26. I have not found evidence that societies that borrowed from Roman law ever received the *senatus consultum Silanianum*.

27. For a few examples from judges see Alan Watson, "A House of Lords' Judgment and Other Tales of the Absurd," *American Journal of Comparative Law* 33 (1985): 673ff. A splendid recent example comes from the Republic of South Africa in 1988: *Du Plessis NO v. Strauss* 1988 (2) SA 105. For lawyers' argumentation produced for the benefit of judges, see Alan Watson, *The Evolution of Law* (Baltimore, 1985), pp. 98ff.; "The Evolution of Law: continued," *Law and History Review* 5 (1987): 537ff. at pp. 566ff.

28. *An Introduction to the Study of the Roman Law* (Boston, 1854), p. 129.

29. See Watson, *Sources of Law*, passim.

30. Tony Honoré, *Tribonian* (London, 1978), p. xiv, considers Tribonian a great jurist, but this opinion reflects the author's inability to distinguish between the work and the role of a jurist and of a legal bureaucrat close to an autocrat.

31. For typical examples of exaggeration of the political impact on judging see David Kairys, *The Politics of Law* (New York, 1982), pp. 3ff.; Ronald Dworkin, *A Matter of Principle* (Cambridge, 1985), pp. 9ff.

32. 1.9, 13*pr.* 19.1; 2.1.*pr.* (which states generally that cases involving feudal law are resolved variously by Roman law, statutes of the Lombards, and custom), 3.1, 9*pr.*, 9.4, 16, 22*pr.*, 24.12, 27, 33.3, 34*pr.*, 38 (custom sanctioned by statute), 39.2, 40, 44*pr.*, 52, 53, 55, 57, 58.1, 58.2, 58.3, 58.4, 58.5. Where texts cannot be compared, there can be no sure way of measuring preceding legislation. Sometimes the preceding legislation is not expressly mentioned. Sometimes authority is given to a text by a reference to nonexistent legislation. To take an example from a different work: paragraph 2 of the prologue of the *Assizes of Romania*, the law code of Frankish Morea of the early fourteenth century (but probably resting in part on a shorter compilation of the thirteenth century), claims that it is based on the usages and customs of Jerusalem (i.e., Constantinople). It seems in fact not to derive from the *Assizes de Jérusalem* as it now exists, and the issue is whether it was based on a now lost earlier version. P. W. Topping gives a negative answer: "The formation of the Assizes of Romania," *Byzantion* 17 (1944–5):304. J. L. La Monte prefers the positive: "Three Questions Concerning the Assizes de Jerusalem," *Byzantina-Metabyzantina* 1 (1946): 201ff. at p. 210f.

33. "Fontes *iuris feudalis Germanici* communis *sunt Ius* feudale Longobardicum, *per Germaniam receptum,* consuetudines Germaniae feudales *universales,* iura imperii communia, *in sanctionibus Imperii, in iure Romano et Canonico comprehensa*" (1.1.10).

34. For a few statements to that effect, see Craig, *Jus Feudale,* 1.9.36.; the Saxon S. Stryk, *Examen Iuris Feudalis,* 1.26; the Prussian Henricus Coccejus, *Juris Feudalis Hypomnemata,* 1.13.

35. 1.5, 6.

36. See Robinson, *Introduction,* p. 61.

37. See Marc Bloch, *Feudal Society* (Chicago, 1961), pp. 48ff.

38. See Adhémerd Esmein, *Précis élémentaire de l'histoire du droit français de 1789 à 1814* (Paris, 1911), pp. 57ff.

39. Chapter 32.

40. See Stryk, *Examen*, 1.15.

41. See Gudelinus, *De Iure Feudorum, prol.* 5.

42. Jason, *Super Usibus Feudalis*, 2 (*in fine*).

43. Stryk, *Examen*, 1.14: "*Ex recepto; quatenus scilicet quodam arbitrio, sciente et non contradicente imperatore in scholas deductae, explicatae, et communi iudiciorum comprobatae.*" He gives references to some who share his opinion.

44. Zoesius, *Praelectiones*, proem. 15; see also Coccejus, *Hypomnemata*, 1.12.

45. See Alan Watson, *Making of the Civil Law* (Cambridge, Mass., 1981), pp. 64ff.

46. See Alan Watson, "Legal Change, Sources of Law and Legal Culture," *University of Pennsylvania Law Review* 131 (1983): 121ff. at p. 1128.

2. SLAVE LAW AND MANUMISSION AT ROME

1. More surprisingly, as I have argued elsewhere, the social institution of slavery had very little impact on the development of Roman private law ("Slavery and the Development of Roman Private Law," *Bullettino dell' Istituto di Diritto Romano* [1987]). Two writers have expressed different opinions. For J. G. Wolf, the ancient Roman action claiming ownership, the *legis actio sacramento in rem*, was designed only for claiming slaves ("Zur legis actio sacramento in rem," in *Römisches Recht in der europäischen Tradition*, O. Behrends, M. Diesselhorst, and W. E. Voss, eds. [Ebelsbach, 1985], 1ff. at pp. 27ff. and 38f). He argues that the process was modeled on delict. A handling, dealing, or touching that was not allowed occurred when one of the claimants wrongfully touched the slave with the staff (*vindicta*). Even if one accepts this account, it would not permit the conclusion that the process was appropriate only where slaves were claimed. One could equally wrongfully touch a bull with a staff. Astonishingly, Orlando Patterson claims that the Romans invented the legal fiction of absolute ownership, *dominium*, to define slaves (*Slavery and Social Death* [Cambridge, Mass., 1982], pp. 30ff.). His argument is incomprehensible to me, but it is at least

certain that he has produced no evidence. He also claims (p. 32) that the "etymology of the word *dominium* further supports our hypothesis. When the word *dominus* first appeared in the third century B.C. it did not mean owner but, significantly, slavemaster." The etymology is unlikely: *dominus* derives from *domus*, *house*, and means *head of a house*; see Alfred Ernout and Arnold Meillet, *Dictionnaire étymologique de la langue latine*, 4th ed. (Paris, 1959), p. 183; A. Walde and J. B. Hofmann, *Lateinisches Etymologisches Wörterbuch*, 5th ed. (Heidelberg, 1982), 1:367: *Oxford Latin Dictionary* (Oxford, 1982), p. 571.

2. See, e.g., Francis De Zulueta, *The Institutes of Gaius* (Oxford, 1953), 2:5.

3. See Keith Hopkins, *Conquerors and Slaves* (Cambridge, 1978), p. 9, and the works cited.

4. For all the foregoing see Alan Watson, "Slavery and the Development of Roman Private Law."

5. The so-called classical forms of manumission are discussed later in this chapter.

6. See Alan Watson, *Roman Slave Law* (Baltimore, 1987), pp. 43 ff.

7. See, e.g., *J.1.6pr.*

8. Whatever the reason for these restrictions may have been, it could not have been to keep down the number of "foreign"-born (Watson, *Roman Slave Law*, p. 31).

9. *J.1.7.1.*

10. Logically, though, the Romans held that a Roman captured by an enemy became a foreign slave and hence lost his Roman citizenship (Watson, *Roman Slave Law*, pp. 20ff).

11. See ibid., pp. 90f.

12. In some cases manumission was by will, conditional upon the slave paying the heir a certain sum from his *peculium*, and in such circumstances the heir was not allowed to obstruct the fulfillment of the condition.

13. *D.33.7.19.1.*

14. "Servus pecuniam ob libertatem pactus erat et eam domino dederat: dominus prius quam eum manumitteret, mortuus erat testamentoque liberum esse iusserat et ei peculium suum legaverat. consulebat, quam pecuniam domino dedisset ob libertatem, an eam sibi heredes patroni reddere deberent necne. respondit, si eam pecuniam dominus, posteaquam accepisset, in suae pecuniae rationem habuisset, statim desisse eius peculii esse: sed si interea, dum eum manumitteret, acceptum servo rettulisset, videri peculii fuisse et debere heredes eam pecuniam manumisso reddere."

15. See Thomas Wiedemann, *Greek and Roman Slavery* (Baltimore, 1981), p. 528.

16. See Alan Watson, "The Identity of Sarapio, Socrates, Longus and Nilus in the Will of C. Longinus Castor," *Irish Jurist* (1966): 313ff.

17. The form of manumission known as *vindicta*.

18. "4. Eadem lege Aelia Sentia domino minori annis viginti non aliter manumittere permittitur, quam si vindicta apud consilium iusta causa manumissionis adprobata fuerint manumissi. 5. Iustae autem manumissionis causae sunt, veluti si quis patrem aut matrem aut filium filiamve aut fratrem sororemve naturales aut paedagogum, nutricem, educatorem aut alumnum alumnamve aut collactaneum manumittat, aut servum procuratoris habendi gratia, aut ancillam matrimonii causa, dum tamen intra sex menses uxor ducatur, nisi iusta causa impediat, et qui manumittitur procuratoris habendi gratia, ne minor septem et decem annis manumittatur."

19. G.1.19.

20. C.6.27.5.1. (531 A.D.); J.2.14.1.

21. C6.4.4.3 (531 A.D.).

22. Since, again, slaves could own nothing, a legacy of his *peculium* to one's own slave would be valid only if the slave was also given his freedom.

23. "4.24.4. Ἀλλ᾽ οὐκ ἐν τοῖς καθ᾽ ἡμᾶς χρόνοις οὕτω ταῦτ᾽ ἔχει, ἀλλ᾽ εἰς τοσαύτην σύγχυσιν ἥκει τὰ πράγματα καὶ τὰ καλὰ τῆς Ῥωμαίων πόλεως οὕτως ἄτιμα καὶ ῥυπαρὰ γέγονεν, ὥσθ᾽ οἱ μὲν ἀπὸ λῃστείας καὶ τοιχωρυχίας καὶ πορνείας καὶ παντὸς ἄλλου πονηροῦ πόρου χρηματισάμενοι τούτων ὠνοῦνται τῶν χρημάτων τὴν ἐλευθερίαν καὶ εὐθύς εἰσι Ῥωμαῖοι· 5. οἱ δὲ συνίστορες καὶ συνεργοὶ τοῖς δεσπόταις γενόμενοι φαρμακειῶν καὶ ἀνδροφονιῶν καὶ τῶν εἰς θεοὺς ἢ τὸ κοινὸν ἀδικημάτων ταύτας φέρονται παρ᾽ αὐτῶν τὰς χάριτας· οἱ δ᾽ ἵνα τὸν δημοσία διδόμενον σῖτον λαμβάνοντες κατὰ μῆνα καὶ εἴ τις ἄλλη παρὰ τῶν ἡγουμένων γίγνοιτο τοῖς ἀπόροις τῶν πολιτῶν φιλανθρωπία φέρωσι τοῖς δεδωκόσι τὴν ἐλευθερίαν· οἱ δὲ διὰ κουφότητα τῶν δεσποτῶν καὶ κενὴν δοξοκοπίαν. 6. ἔγωγ᾽ οὖν ἐπίσταμαί τινας ἅπασι τοῖς δούλοις συγκεχωρηκότας εἶναι ἐλευθέροις μετὰ τὰς ἑαυτῶν τελευτάς, ἵνα χρηστοὶ καλῶνται νεκροὶ καὶ πολλοὶ ταῖς κλίναις αὐτῶν ἐκκομιζομέναις παρακολουθῶσι τοὺς πίλους ἔχοντες ἐπὶ ταῖς κεφαλαῖς· ἐν οἷς ἐπόμπευόν τινες, ὡς ἦν παρὰ τῶν ἐπισταμένων ἀκούειν, ἐκ τῶν δεσμωτηρίων ἐξεληλυθότες ἀρτίως κακοῦργοι μυρίων ἄξια διαπεπραγμένοι θανάτων. εἰς τούτους μέντοι τοὺς δυσεκκαθάρτους σπίλους¹ ἐκ τῆς πόλεως ἀποβλέποντες οἱ πολλοὶ δυσχεραίνουσι καὶ προβέβληνται τὸ ἔθος, ὡς οὐ

πρέπον ἡγεμονικῇ πόλει καὶ παντὸς ἄρχειν ἀξιούσῃ τόπου τοιούτους ποιεῖσθαι πολίτας."

24. Livy 41.9.11; see also Alan Watson, *The Law of Persons in the Later Roman Republic* (Oxford, 1967), pp. 165f., 192.

25. See F. B. Marsh, *History of the Roman World, 146 to 30 B.C.*, 3d ed. by H. H. Scullard (London, 1963), p. 98.

26. C.7.3.1.1.

27. C.7.6.2.

28. C.7.3.1.5.

29. C.7.3.1.9.

30. C.1.13.1, 2.

31. *D*.22.5.22.1; *C*.9.41.12; 9.41.15; 9.41.18; *Pauli Senteniae* 5.16.1.; see Watson, *Roman Slave Law*, pp. 84ff.

32. *D*48.2.12.3; see Watson, *Roman Slave Law*, pp. 129ff.

33. *C. Th.* 9.6.2. (376 A.D.).

34. *C. Th.* 9.5.1.1 (320–23 A.D.).

35. *C. Th.* 9.6.2.

36. *Epitome Ulpiani* 5.5.

37. "In potestate itaque dominorum sunt servi. quae quidem potestas iuris gentium est: nam apud omnes peraeque gentes animadvertere possumus, dominis in servos vitae necisque potestatem esse, et quodcumque per servum adquiritur id domino adquiritur. 2. Sed hoc tempore nullis hominibus qui sub imperio nostro sunt licet sine causa legibus cognita et supra modum in servos suos saevire. nam ex constitutione divi Pii Antonini qui sine causa servum suum occiderit, non minus puniri iubetur quam qui servum alienum occiderit. sed et maior asperitas dominorum eiusdem principis constitutione coercetur. nam consultus a quibusdam praesidibus provinciarum de his servis qui ad aedem sacram vel ad statuas principum confugiunt, praecepit, ut si intolerabilis videatur dominorum saevitia, cogantur servos bonis condicionibus vendere, ut pretium dominis daretur: et recte; expedit enim rei publicae, ne quis re sua male utatur. cuius rescripti ad Aelium Marcianum emisi verba haec sunt: 'Dominorum quidem potestatem in suos servos illibatam esse oportet nec cuiquam hominum ius suum detrahi. sed dominorum interest, ne auxilium contra saevitiam vel famem vel intolerabilem iniuriam denegetur his qui iuste deprecantur. ideoque cognosce de querellis eorum qui ex familia Iulii Sabini ad statuam confugerunt, et si vel durius habitos quam aequum est, vel infami iniuria affectos cognoveris, veniri iube, ita ut in potestatem domini non revertantur. qui Sabinus, si meae constitutioni fraudem fecerit, sciet, me admissum severius exsecuturum.' "

38. See W. W. Buckland, *The Roman Law of Slavery* (Cambridge, 1908), p. 38.

39. For restrictions on the master's right to ill-treat slaves see Watson, *Roman Slave Law*, pp. 115ff.

40. *C. Th.* 9.6.2.

41. *D.*9.2.

42. *D*47.10.15.34 to end; see Watson, *Roman Slave Law*, pp. 61ff.

43. See *D.*9.1.

44. *C.*9.9.23.

45. See, e.g., *D.*23.2.14.2; 2.4.4.3; *J.*3.6.10.

46. "Plerumque propter morbosa mancipia etiam non morbosa redhibentur, si separari non possint sine magno incommodo vel ad pietatis rationem offensam. quid enim, si filio retento parentes redhibere maluerint vel contra? quod et in fratribus et in personas contubernio sibi coniunctas observari oportet."

47. "Possessionum divisiones sic fieri oportet, ut integra apud successorem unumquemque servorum vel colonorum adscripticiae condicionis seu inquilinorum proxima agnatio vel adfinitas permaneret. quis enim ferat liberos a parentibus, a fratribus sorores, a viris coniuges segregari? igitur si qui dissociata in ius diversum mancipia vel colonos traxerint, in unum eadem redigere cogantur."

48. A commonplace of many writers on slavery is that the laws and customs of slave societies give evidence of the essential contradiction of thinking of human beings as things; see David B. Davis, *The Problem of Slavery in Western Culture* (Ithaca, 1966), pp. 57, 62.

49. See *Politics* 1.4–6.

50. *D.*21.1.1.1; 21.1.17.14.

51. *C.*6.1.4.4 (317 A.D.).

52. *C.*6.1.6.

53. 11.4.1.1.

54. See above all, David Daube, "Slave-Catching," *Juridical Review* 64 (1952): 12ff.

55. *C.*1.1.0.1 (339 A.D.). For circumcising a slave a Jew would be put to death and the slave would be freed.

56. *C.*1.10.2; 1.3.54(56).8(3).

57. *G.*3.40–44; see Watson, *Roman Slave Law*, pp. 35ff.

58. *D.*38.1.15*pr.*; 38.1.16*pr.*, 1; 38.1.46; 38.1.48.2. See, most recently, W. Waldstein, *Operae Libertorum: Untersuchungen zur Dienstpflicht freigelassener Sklaven* (Stuttgart, 1986).

59. See Watson, *Roman Slave Law*, pp. 39ff.

60. "Imperatoris Commodi constitutio talis profertur: 'Cum probatum sit contumeliis patronos a libertis esse violatos vel illata manu atroci esse pulsatos aut etiam paupertate vel corporis valetudine laborantes relictos, primum eos in potestate patronorum redigi et ministerium dominis praebere cogi: sin autem nec hoc modo admoneantur, vel a praeside emptori addicentur et pretium patronis tribuetur.' "

61. See Buckland, *Roman Law of Slavery*, pp. 423f.

62. C.6.7.1; 6.3.8; 6.3.2.

63. C7.17.1. In previous law, there was a need for someone else to make the claim or defend on behalf of the slave. But any person competent to appear in court could accept that role.

64. "Non est dubitatum cogi posse heredem institutum adire et restituere hereditatem servis, sive directa sive fideicommissaria libertas eis data fuisset, cum aspernari heres non deberet personam cogentis: habet enim hic quoque aditum, ut, qui nondum petere fideicommissariam libertatem possit nec directam sibi vindicare, propter spem tamen libertatis et hereditatis aditum ad praetorem et per se habeat."

65. "Sed et si servus heres institutus fuerit, si nemo natus sit, Aristo scribit, huic quoque servo quamvis non omnia, quaedam tamen circa partum custodiendum arbitrio praetoris esse concedenda. quam sententiam puto veram: publice enim interest partus non subici, ut ordinum dignitas familiarumque salva sit: ideoque etiam servus iste, cum sit in spe constitutus successionis, qualisqualis sit, debet audiri rem et publicam et suam gerens."

66. *D.*48.8.4.2. Some details of Roman law, whose importance for us lies in their subsequent development, are treated in Chapter 3.

67. See, e.g., *D.*13.7.43.1; 18.6.13.2; 18.6.14; 19.2.13.8; 47.11.6.2; 50.4.1.2.

68. Until Justinian, things were classed either as *res mancipi* (which included slaves) or *res nec mancipi*, and the former required specific formalities for transfer. Justinian abolished the distinction in C.7.31.1.5, and thereafter no particular form was required for the alienation of slaves.

3. SLAVE LAW IN SPAIN AND SPANISH AMERICA

1. See Alvaro d'Ors, *Estudios visigóticos, II: El código de Eurico* (Rome, 1960).

2. A. García Gallo, "Nacionalidad y territorialidad del derecho en la

época visigoda," *Anuario de Historia del Derecho Español* 13 (1941): 168ff. at p. 194; d'Ors, *Estudios, II*, pp. 6ff. For arguments to the contrary see Alan Watson, *The Evolution of Law* (Baltimore, 1986), p. 82.

3. Watson, *Evolution*, pp. 91f.

4. 5.7.9, 10, 17, 20.

5. And see the rules in 3.2.3 and 4.

6. 2.4.9.

7. 5.4.14.

8. 5.7.11.

9. 5.7.12.

10. See C. Verlinden, *L'Esclavage dans l'Europe médiévale* (Bruges, 1955), 1:147ff.

11. *J.*1.3.2.

12. 4.22*pr*. The matter is further dealt with in Chapter 8.

13. *J.*1.5.1.

14. *J.*1.6.7.

15. 4.22.1.

16. 4.22.5.

17. 4.22.6. In some circumstances a slave who became a cleric without the knowledge of his master would be freed if he provided a substitute slave (or two if he became a bishop).

18. 6.3.21.

19. 6.3.24.

20. 6.16.7.

21. 6.4.23.

22. 4.21.8.

23. 4.22.9.

24. 7.8.9.

25. 4.21.7.

26. *J.*2.1.29–34; D.41.1.7.1, 3, 10, 12, 13; 41.1.10 *pr*. 1, 2.

27. See J. Manzano Manzano, *La Incorporación de las Indias a la Corona de Castilla* (Madrid, 1948), *passim*, esp. pp. 351ff.; Francisco Tómas y Valiente, *Manual de historia del derecho español*, 4th ed. (Madrid, 1983), p. 330.

28. By royal order of 12 April 1495 they were to be sold in Andalucia, but subsequently by royal order of 20 June 1500 they were to be freed and returned to their native land (Documents 2 and 5 in Richard Konetzke, *Colección de documentos para la historia de la formación social de Hispanoamerica, 1493–1810* [Madrid, 1953], 1:2, 4).

29. See Alan Watson, *Legal Transplants: An Approach to Comparative Law* (Edinburgh, 1976).

30. A ruling of the Emperor Charles V of 9 November 1526 to that effect makes clear that the law was already settled; it is in the *Recopilación*, 6.2.1.

31. See Tómas y Valiente, *Manual*, pp. 325ff.

32. Document no. 185 in Konetzke, *Colección de Documentos*, 1:185.

33. Document no. 41 in ibid., pp. 81f.

34. The text is reproduced by Raúl Carrancá y Trujillo, "El estatuto jurídico de los esclavos en las postrimeriás de la colonización española," *Revista de Historia de América* 3 (1938): 20ff. at pp. 50ff. It is also document no. 308 in Konetzke, *Colección*, 3 (Madrid, 1962), pp. 643ff.

35. Cap. 7. This decree even provides for the purchase of one slave if the estates of the two masters are distant.

36. Cap. 1.

37. Cap. 2. A state that has laws regulating the provision of clothing and so on to slaves is not necessarily more humane than a state that has no such law. The existence of laws may indicate a need for them, whereas in other states it was accepted as a given that a minimum standard of care of slaves was needed. See David Daube, "The Self-Understood in Legal History" *Juridical Review* 18 (1973): 126ff.

38. Cap. 3.

39. Cap. 4.

40. Cap. 5.

41. Cap. 8.

42. Cap. 9.

43. Cap. 10.

44. Cap. 11.

45. Cap. 13.

46. This is not expressly stated, but the text talks of notice "dada por el eclesiástico por razón de su ministerio o por queja de los esclavos" ("given by the priest from his ministry or from complaint of the slaves"). The notice to the *procurador síndico* is by the priest, the complaint of the slaves is to the priest.

47. The document is no. 204 in Konetzke, *Colección*, 3:337ff. Indeed, the Spanish crown raised tax money in various ways from slavery and the slave trade; see, e.g., J. P. Tardieu, *Le Destin des noirs aux Indes de Castile, XVIe–XVIIIe siècles* (Paris, 1986), pp. 122ff.

48. The document is no. 212 in Konetzke, *Colección*, 3:360ff.

49. No. 308 in ibid., pp. 643ff.

50. No. 280 in ibid., p. 553.

51. Hans Baade, "The Law of Slavery in Spanish Louisiana, 1769–1803," in E. F. Haas, ed., *Louisiana's Legal Heritage* (Pensacola, 1983), p. 46. More surprisingly, he claims that David B. Davis, *The Problem of Slavery in Western Culture* (Ithaca, 1966), p. 267, had written that it did not apply in Spanish Santo Domingo.

52. Davis, *Problem*, p. 267.

53. *Epitome Ulpiani* 2.4.; *D.*40.1.25; 40.1.29.1.

54. *D.*18.7.

55. Tardieu, *Destin*, pp. 255ff.

56. Arrangements by which a slave is allowed to earn and keep money as if it belongs to the slave are found elsewhere. Thus, for South Carolina, Mary Boykin Chesnut, *A Diary from Dixie*, ed. B. A. Williams (Cambridge, Mass., 1980), writes of a seamstress, Martha, who hired out her own time, paying her owner five dollars a month (p. 162), and of a poultry business run by another slave, Molly, with a percentage going to the mistress (p. 165). For Georgia, Frances Anne Kemble, *Journal of a Residence on a Georgian Plantation in 1838–1839*, ed. J. A. Scott (Athens, Ga., 1984), p. 73, tells of slaves trading in poultry, moss, and eggs for their own advantage.

57. "Si quis dicat se suis nummis emptum, potest consistere cum domino suo, cuius in fidem confugit, et queri, quod ab eo non manumittatur, Romae quidem apud praefectum urbis, in provinciis vero apud praesides ex sacris constitutionibus divorum fratrum."

58. See Tardieu, *Destin*, p. 245.

59. Ibid. pp. 258ff.

60. Ibid., pp. 60ff.

61. Ibid., pp. 238f.

62. Ibid., pp. 237ff.

63. Ibid., p. 247.

64. Suetonius, *Deified Claudius*, 25.2; *D.*40.8.2.; *C.*7.6.1.3; see Alan Watson, *Roman Slave Law* (Baltimore, 1987), p. 123.

65. See Tardieu, *Destin*, pp. 249f.

66. Ibid., pp. 178ff.

67. See Konetzke, document no. 9, in *Colección*, 1:9ff.

68. No. 339 in ibid., 3:726ff.

69. See Tardieu, *Destin*, pp. 15f., 100f., 116.

70. Ibid., pp. 184ff., 197.

71. Ibid., pp. 163ff.

72. For the proposition that the French slave population was almost stag-

nant see Gaston Martin, *Histoire de l'esclavage dans les colonies françaises* (Brionne, 1948), pp. 124ff. For Guadelupe see Nicole Vanony-Frisch, *Les Esclaves de la Guadelupe à la fin de l'Ancien Régime d'après les sources notariales, 1770–1789* (Guadelupe, 1985), pp. 57ff.

73. See Javier Malagón Barceló, *Código Negro Carolino 1784* (Santo Domingo, R.D., 1974), p. xli.

74. Ibid., pp. xliiif.

75. Ibid., pp. li, lxi.

76. C. A. Palmer, dealing with slavery in Mexico, also stresses that laws made in the colonies were more repressive for slaves than were *Las Siete Partidas*. But the rules he cites deal only with punishment of slaves and the rounding up of runaways (*Slaves of the White God* [Cambridge, Mass., 1976], pp. 5, 119ff.).

77. For details, see Tardieu, *Destin*, pp. 107ff.

78. Document no. 274 (of 30 April 1557) in Konetzke, *Colección*, 1:361.

79. See ibid., 2:61, 259, 280; 3:247.

80. Document no. 96 in ibid., 3:137f.

81. Ibid., 3:201, 331, 340.

82. Ibid., p. 265.

83. For a study of slave law in a particular geographical area, corresponding to modern Argentina and Paraguay, see A. Levaggi, "La condición juridica del esclavo en la epoca hispanica," *Revista de Historia del Derecho* 1 (1973): 83ff.

4. ENGLAND AND SLAVE LAW IN AMERICA

1. In 1547 enslavement was introduced into England by the statute 1 Edw. VI c.3 as punishment for vagabonds. The statute claims that idleness and "vagabundrye" were the mother of all thefts, robberies, and other evil acts. The statute was a failure and was repealed two years later. It was a commonplace throughout western Europe that the disappearance of slavery was the cause of healthy beggars and robberies. See S. Pufendorf, *De Jure Naturae et Gentium*, 6.3.10.

2. *Commentaries on the Laws of England* (first published 1765), 1:105.

3. But from 15 December 1614, laws of Castile were not law in America unless they were passed by the Consejo de las Indias (*Recopilación de las Indias*, 2.1.39, 40).

4. H. S. Klein stresses the strenuous efforts of the Castilian monarchy to keep control in Spanish colonies, he observes that Castilian law was applied in its entirety, and he draws a contrast with England and its colonies (*Slavery in the Americas: A Comparative Study of Virginia and Cuba* [Chicago, 1967], pp. 57ff.). But he seems to overlook the fundamental point that this difference was inherent in the two legal traditions.

5. See, for the West Indies, James Stephen, *Slavery of the British West India Colonies* (London, 1824), 1:14. For slave law in the British West Indies in general see that work and "General View of the Principles on which this System of Laws appears to have been Originally Founded" in (U.K.) *House of Commons Accounts and Papers* (1789), vol. 26, no. 646a, pt. 3 (available on microform).

6. For an excellent short account of the law in the various states of the United States see William Goodell, *The American Slave Code* (1853, rpt. New York, 1968). See also Paul Finkelman, *The Law of Freedom and Bondage* (New York, 1986). For statutes on slavery see William M. Wiecek, "The Statutory Law of Slavery and Race in the Thirteen Mainland Colonies of British America," *William and Mary Quarterly* 3d ser., 34 (1977): 258ff.

7. See Michael H. Hoeflich, "American Judges and Roman Law," 8 *Law and History Review* (1990).

8. First published in 1812.

9. See, e.g., *Bynum* v. *Walker*, 4 Desaussure 206 (Philadelphia 1854) (1812); *Milledge* v. *Lamar*, Desaussure 617 (Philadelphia 1884) (1817); *Gregg* v. *Thompson*, 2 Mill. 331 (1818); *Wingis* v. *Smith*, 3 McCord 400 (1825); *Tidyman* v. *Rose*, Rich. Eq. Cas. 294 (1832); *Fable* v. *Brown*, 2 Hill Eq. 378 (1835); *Bowers* v. *Newman*, 2 McMullan 472 (1842); *McLeish* v. *Burch*, 3 Strob. Eq. 225 (1849); *Belcher* v. *McKelvey*, 11 Rich. Eq. 9 (1859).

10. See, to much the same effect, *Fable* v. *Brown*.

11. See, e.g., *Fable* v. *Brown*.

12. I should spell out what I mean by private law. The distinction between private law and public law goes back at least to early Rome, but the dividing line is difficult to draw: see J. A. C. Thomas, *The Institutes of Justinian* (Cape Town, 1975), p. 3, on *J*.1.1.4. Here I use the term *private law* to cover the topics one would expect to find in a modern European civil code: persons, obligations, property, succession. Likewise, within a branch of the law such as contract I am excluding from the notion of private law issues that would not be dealt with in a civil code or, say, an English textbook on contract that was intended for the use of law students.

13. For slave law in South Carolina see in general John Belton O'Neall, *The Negro Law of South Carolina* (Columbia, 1848); H. M. Henry, *The Police Control of the Slave in South Carolina* (1914; rpt. New York, 1968).

14. See P. H. Wood, *Black Majority* (New York, 1975).

15. See ibid., pp. 35ff.

16. *Statutes at Large of South Carolina*, 1 (Columbia, 1836), p. 55. At this time North and South Carolina were one province. The formal division occurred in 1729, but they had practically different governments after 1690.

17. Provisions from the 95th onward declare that no one can be a freeman of Carolina unless he acknowledges a God, but that any religion, even non-Christian, may be professed.

18. Probably together with the Earl of Shaftesbury.

19. *Acts, passed in the Island of Barbados from 1643, to 1762, inclusive* (London, 1764), no. 82, pp. 112ff.

20. See also sections 2 and 8 of the 1712 Act for the Better Ordering and Governing of Negroes and Slaves; sections 2, 5, and 7 of the 1722 Act for the better Ordering and Governing of Negroes and other Slaves; section 2 of the 1735 act; and sections 3 and 36 of the 1740 Act for the better Ordering and Governing of Negroes and other Slaves in this Province.

21. See also section 26 of the 1735 Act, and section 33 of the 1740 act.

22. See also section 31 of the 1735 act, and section 34 of the 1740 act.

23. See also section 40 of the 1740 act.

24. See David Daube, *Roman Law: Linguistic, Social and Philosophical Aspects* (Edinburgh, 1969), pp. 124ff.

25. A similar fear was felt in some Spanish colonies.

26. Judge John Belton O'Neall in *The Negro Law of South Carolina* expresses disapproval of some legal rules and suggests reforms. Most of the rules he objects to are those which contain this public dimension. For instance, he wished owners to have the regulated right to manumit slaves and to make bequests to them (1.37–44). He objected to the prohibition against teaching slaves to read or write (2.42); to the regulating of slaves' clothing, a provision he says had never been enforced (2.49); and to the prohibition against a master or overseer permitting his slaves to beat drums or blow horns (2.57). Above all, he says at 2.35: "The right of the master, to provide as comfortably as he pleases for his slave, could not be and ought not to be abridged in the present state of public opinion. The law may very well compel a master to furnish his slave with proper, necessary, wholesome and abundant raiment and food; but certainly no legislator now would venture

to say to a master, you shall not allow your slave to have a canoe to fish with, or to carry vegetables to market or that he should not be allowed to have a horse to attend to his duties as a stock-minder in the swamps, savannas, and pine forests of the lower part of the State, or that a family of slaves should not have a cow to furnish them with milk, or a hog to make for them meat, beyond their usual allowance. All these are matters between the master and the slave in which neither the public nor any prying, meddling, mischievous neighbor, has any thing to do. Experience and observation fully satisfy me that the first law of slavery is that of kindness from the master to the slave. With that properly inculcated, enforced by law and judiciously applied, slavery becomes a family relation, next in its attachments to that of parent and child." O'Neall's proposals were disapproved of by the Committee of the Judiciary to which they were referred. On O'Neall see A. E. Keir Nash, "Negro Rights, Unionism, and Greatness of the South Carolina Court of Appeals: The Extraordinary Chief Justice John Belton O'Neall," *South Carolina Law Review* 21 (1969): 141ff.

27. Thus there could also be no valid marriage between a free black and a slave, with the consequence that any children were illegitimate and could not inherit from the free parent. Judge O'Neall suggested "a judicious enactment to remedy it" (*Negro Law of South Carolina*, 2.35).

28. Judge O'Neall proposed that punishment of slaves and free blacks should be much more restricted and that the right of appeal in noncapital cases should be granted, and he protested vehemently against the tribunal for trial, which he described as "the worst system which could be devised" (*Negro Law of South Carolina*, 3.31, 32).

29. See also the act of 1712, section 17; act of 1722, section 18; act of 1740, section 24.

30. See also the act of 1712, section 12.

31. Section 5 of the act of 1714.

32. See, e.g., act of 1740, section 16; act of 1751, section 7.

33. See also the act of 1712, section 34.

34. It was presumed that blacks were slaves; act of 1722, section 1; act of 1740, section 1.

35. 14 Rich. Eq. 90.

36. *McLeish* v. *Burch* 3 Strob. Eq. 225 (1849).

37. 3 Rich. Eq. 262.

38. 10 Richardson 465.

39. *Johnson* v. *Clarkson*, 7 Rich. Eq. 305 (1851).

40. See, e.g., *Linam* v. *Johnson*, 2 Bailey 137 (1831); *Cline* v. *Caldwell* 1

Hill 423 (1833); *Blackman v. Gordon*, 2 Rich. Eq. 43 (1845); *Guillemette v. Harper*, 4 Richardson 186 (1850); *Miller v. Mitchell*, Bailey Eq. 437 (1831) *Broughton v. Telfer*, 3 Rich. Eq. 431 (1851).

41. 2 McMullan 454 (1842).

42. P. 464.

43. 11 Rich. Eq. 447 (1860).

44. See also *Farr v. Thompson*, 1 Richardson 81, Cheves 37. The case is particularly interesting in that Farr's first will of 1828 gave his whole estate to Judge J. B. O'Neall as executor, and that a letter three days later to the judge declared that he wished the beneficiaries to be Fun, his slave and mistress, and Henry, his slave and son, and that he wanted them to be free.

45. South Carolina is, of course, not the only state in which white fathers went to extreme lengths to free their slave children and to evade prohibitions on manumission. For Mississippi, for instance, see *Shaw v. Brown*, 35 Miss. 246 (1858) and *Mitchell v. Wells*, 37 Miss. 235 (1859). These cases are discussed by Paul Finkelman, *An Imperfect Union* (Chapel Hill, 1981), pp. 232ff. and 287ff. respectively.

46. See, e.g., the wills from Georgia cited by J. F. Smith, *Slavery and Rice Culture in Low Country Georgia, 1750–1860* (Knoxville, 1985), pp. 199ff.

47. For the Stono uprising and a discussion of the 1740 act see Wood, *Black Majority*, pp. 308ff., esp. p. 324.

5. FRANCE AND SLAVE LAW IN AMERICA

1. See Jean Bodin, *Les Six livres de la république* (first published 1579), book 1, chap. 5; Jean Domat, *Les Loix civiles dans leur ordre naturel* (first published between 1689 and 1697), preliminary book, title 2, section 2.

2. For a longer discussion see Alan Watson, *Sources of Law, Legal Change, and Ambiguity* (Philadelphia, 1984), pp. 40ff., 68ff.

3. See, e.g., *Lettres patentes pour l'établissement de la Compagnie Royale de Saint Domingue* of September 1695, cap. 23; *Code noir*, p. 131, article 42 of the royal edict of March 1724 for Louisiana, *Code noir*, p. 347; for Quebec, *Commission of Jacques Duchesneau, Intendant*, June 1675 (rpt. in J.-G. Castel, *The Civil Law System of the Province of Quebec* (Toronto, 1962), pp. 12ff.

4. Thus it would be difficult to claim that this part of Roman law was the written law of France or even the common law of France since it obviously had not been received. To accept it as written reason also would cause prob-

lems because one could not claim that it was in harmony with the spirit of the customs.

5. For the *Code noir* see in general Louis Sala-Molins, *Le code noir ou le calvaire de Canaan* (Paris, 1987). For the background to the drafting of the royal edict of March 1685 see Lucien Peytraud, *L'Esclavage aux Antilles françaises avant 1789* (Paris, 1984), 1:182ff.

6. Article 33 of the royal edict of March 1685 for the islands; *Code noir*, p. 44, article 27 of the royal edict of March 1724 for Louisiana; *Code noir*, p. 339.

7. *Code noir*, p. 45.

8. See J. A. C. Thomas, *Textbook of Roman Law* (Amsterdam, 1976), pp. 381–82.

9. There is a variation from Roman law in that the owner had three days from condemnation to exercise his option whereas at Rome the master had to decide to surrender before condemnation.

10. *Code noir*, pp. 340f.

11. "Les Maistres âgez de vingt ans pourront affranchir leurs Esclaves par tous Actes entre-vifs ou à cause de mort, sans qu'ils soient tenus de rendre raison de leur affranchissement, ny qu'ils ayent besoin d'avis de parens, encore qu'ils soient mineurs de vingt-cinq ans" (ibid., pp. 55f.). Royal ordinances of 15 December 1721 and of 1 February 1741 forbade minors under twenty-five, even if emancipated, from freeing their slaves.

12. "Les enfans qui auront esté faits légataires universels par leurs Maistres, ou nommez Executeurs de leurs Testamens, ou Tuteurs de leurs enfans, seront tenus & réputez, & les tenons & réputons pour affranchis" (ibid., p. 56).

13. Ibid., pp. 56f.

14. Ibid., p. 57.

15. See Thomas, *Textbook*, p. 404.

16. *Code noir*, pp. 352ff.

17. See D. E. Everett, "Free Persons of Color in Colonial Louisiana," *Louisiana History* 7 (1966): 21ff. at pp. 29ff.

18. See Etienne Pasquier, *L'Interprétation des Institutes de Justinian*, 1.26. (Pasquier was born in 1529 and died in 1615, but this work was not published until 1847). Antoine Loisel (1536–1617), *Institutes Coutumières*, 1.1.72, 73, 74.

19. Pasquier, *L'Interprétation*, 1.27; Loisel, *Institutes*, 1.1.73. A similar provision is also to be found in some other countries, for example, Scotland: *Regiam Majestatem*, 2.1.4.5.

20. *Code noir*, p. 354.

21. Ibid., pp. 354f.

22. Ibid., p. 355.

23. The article corresponds to article 6 of the edict of March 1724.

24. "N'entendons toutefois le present Article avoir lieu, lorsque l'homme n'étoit point marié à une autre personne durant son concubinage avec son Esclave, épousera dans les formes observées par l'Eglise ladite Esclave, qui sera affranchie par ce moyen, & les enfans rendus libres & légitimes" (*Code noir*, p. 30).

25. Ibid., pp. 324f.

26. Ibid., p. 48.

27. Ibid., pp. 344f.

28. Ibid., p. 43.

29. Ibid., pp. 337f.

30. Ibid., p. 337.

31. Royal Edict of March 1685, articles 32–38, *Code noir*, pp. 43ff.; edict of March 1724, articles 26–33, *Code noir*, pp. 340ff.

32. Royal edict of March 1685, article 40, *Code noir*, p. 47, edict of March 1724, article 32, *Code noir*, p. 341.

33. *Code noir*, p. 49.

34. Ibid., p. 346.

35. Ibid., pp. 334f.

36. "Voulons neantmoins que les Maistres soient tenus de ce que leurs Esclaves auront fait par leur commandement, ensemble de ce qu'ils auront géré & négocié dans leurs boutiques, & pour l'espece particulier de commerce à laquelle leurs Maistres les auront préposez; & en cas que leurs Maistres n'ayent donné aucun ordre, & ne les ayent point préposez, ils seront tenus seulement jusqu'à concurrence de ce qui aura tourné à leur profit; & si rien n'a tourné au profit des Maistres, le pecule desdits Esclaves que les Maistres leur auront permis d'avoir, en sera tenu, après que leurs Maistres en auront déduit par préférence, ce qui pourra leur en estre dû, sinon, que le pecule consistast en tout ou partie en marchandises dont les Esclaves auroient permission de faire trafic à part, sur lesquelles leurs Maistres viendron seulement par contribution au sol la livre avec les autres Créanciers" (Ibid., pp. 335ff.).

37. Edict of March 1685, articles 1, 2, 3, 4, 5, 6, 7, 8, 14, *Code noir*, pp. 23ff.; edict of October 1716 for the colonies, preamble, *Code noir*, pp. 192ff.; edict of March 1724, articles 1, 2, 3, 4, 5, 6, 10, *Code noir*, pp. 320ff., 326f.

38. But for opposition by planters to Jesuit priests performing marriage ceremonies for their slaves see D'Auberteuil, *Considerations sur la Colonie de S. Domingue*, 2:67f. Until the revocation of the Edict of Nantes in 1724 the only persons (including slaves) who could marry were Catholics; see *Code noir*, p. 29.

39. Edict of March 1685, articles 9, 10, 11, 47, *Code noir*, pp. 29ff., 51; edict of October 1716, article 8, *Code noir*, p. 200; edict of March 1724, articles 6, 7, 8, 9, 43, *Code noir*, pp. 324ff., 348. Also there could not be separate seizure of creditors of husband, wife, and children under puberty: edict of March 1685, article 47, *Code noir*, p. 51; edict of March 1724, article 43, *Code noir*, p. 348.

40. Edict of March 1685, articles 22, 23, 24, 25, 26, 27, *Code noir*, pp. 32ff.; edict of March 1724, articles 20, 21, *Code noir*, pp. 332ff.

41. This ordinance is not contained in the *Code noir*.

42. *Code noir*, pp. 476ff.

43. Berquin Duvallon, *Vue de la colonie espagnole du Mississippi, etc.* (Paris, 1803), pp. 24–25, quoted in *Louisiana under Spain, France and the United States, 1785–1807*, ed. James A. Robertson (Cleveland, 1911), 1:218f.

44. See Peytraud, *Esclavage*, 1:484.

6. PORTUGAL AND SLAVE LAW IN AMERICA

1. See Charles Verlinden, *L'Esclavage dans l'Europe médiévale* (Bruges, 1955), 1:113, 501; P. de Miranda, *Fontes e evoluçao do direito civil brasileiro*, 2d ed. (Rio de Janeiro, 1981), pp. 48ff., claims that after the Reconquista there were no slaves in Portugal but only *adscripti glebae*.

2. See Verlinden, *Esclavage*, 1:615ff.

3. See ibid., pp. 630f.

4. "Quando algum caso fôr trazido em práctica, que seja determinado por alguma Lei de nossos Reinos, ou estilo de nossa Côrte, ou costume nos ditos Reinos, ou em cada uma parte delas longamente usado, e tal, que por Direito se deva guardar, seja por êles julgado, sem embargo do que as Leis Imperiais acêrca do dito caso noutra maneira dispõem; porque onde a Lei, Estilo, ou costume de nossos Reinos dispoem cessem tôdas as outras Leis e Direitos. E quando o caso, de que se trata, não fôr determinado por Lei, Estilo, ou costume de nossos Reinos, mandamos que seja julgado, sendo matéria que traga pecado, pelos Sagrados Cânones. E sendo matéria, que

não traga pecado, seja julgado pelas Leis Imperiais, pôsta que os Sagrados Cânones determinem o contrário. As quais Leis Imperiais mandamos sòmente guardar pela boa razão, em que são fundadas. 1. E se o caso, de que se trata em prática, não fôr determinado por Lei de nosses Reinos, Estilo, ou costume acima dito, ou Leis Imperiais, ou pelos Sagrados Cânones, então mandamos que se guardem as glosas de Acúrsio, incorporadas nas ditas Leis, quando por commum opinião dos Doutores não forem reprovadas; e quando pelas ditas glosas o caso não fôr determinado, segundo a opinião de Bartolo, porque sua opinião comumente é mais conforme à razao, sem embargo que alguns Doutores tivessem o contrário, salvo se a comum opinião dos Doutores que depois dêle escreveram, fôr contrária. 2. E acontecendo caso, ao qual por nenhum dos ditos modos fôsse provido, mandamos que o notifiquem a Nós, para o determinarmos; porque não sãmente tais determinações são desembargo daquele feito, que se trata, mas são Leis para desembargarem outros semelhantes. 3. E sendo o caso, de que se trata tal, que não seja matéria de pecado, e não fôsse determinado por Lei do Reino, nem Estilo do nossa Côrte, nem costume de nossos Reinos, nem Lei Imperial, e fôsse determinado pelos textos dos Cânones, por um modo e pelas glosas e Doutores das Leis por outro modo, mandamos que tal caso seja remetido a Nós, para darmos sôbre isso nossa determinaçao, a qual se guardará."

5. See P. J. Mellius Freirius, *Historiae Juris Civilis Lusitani Liber Singularis*, section 92 (p. 76 in the edition of Coimbra, 1860); Guilherme Braga da Cruz, "A Formaçao historica do moderno direito privado portugûes a Brasileiro," *Revista da Faculdade de Direito de Sao Paolo* 50 (1955): 32ff. at p. 35; Orlando Gomes, "Historical and Sociological Roots of the Brazilian Civil Code," *Inter-American Law Review* 1 (1959): 331f. The historical background of the *Ordenaçoes Filipinas* had some impact. Above all, one should single out two previous collections of laws. The *Ordenaçoes Afonsinas* were published in 1446 in the name of Alfonso V, who was regent for the infant Pedro. The main sources were Roman and canon law, *Las Siete Partidas*, and local customs. Gaps were to be filled from Accursius, failing whom Bartolus. It is noteworthy that João das Regras was a pupil of Bartolus and studied in Bologna. The *Ordenaçoes Manuelinas* of 1515 made few important changes in the law, but, for instance, legal distinctions between Moors and Christians, or between Jews and Christians, disappeared, and a different arrangement for matrimonial property was made. *Ordenaçoes Filipinas* 3.64 (which has just been quoted) on subsidiary sources of law derives directly from *Ordenaçoes Manuelinas*, 2.5 *pr.*, 1, 5.

6. The heading reads: "Quando os que compram escravos ou bestas os poderão enjeitar por doenças ou manqueiras."

7. See *D.*21.1.1.1.

8. See Mellius Freirius, *Historia,* section 92 (p. 77 in the edition of Coimbra, 1860).

9. For the admiration conferred on it, see Mellius Freirius, *Historia,* section 107 (pp. 87f., in the edition of Coimbra, 1860); Gomes, "Historical and Sociological Roots," pp. 332f.

10. "Servitutem cum ratione non pugnare, diximus modo. Ipsis quoque Christianis sero servitus displicuit, nec in sacris literis veteribus aut novis improbatur. Etiam Caroli M. Ludovici Pii, ac Lotharii Leges de servis supersunt in lib. LL. Car. M. et Longob. Imo et Gulielmi Siciliae Regis et Friderici Imp. extant de servis fugitivis constitutiones in plac. Neap. Sed ab hoc tempore, id est, anno Christi CIC CC XII aut non multo secus, Christiani se mutuo in servitium redigere desierunt, quod et Muhammedani ac Turcae inter suos servant, teste Busbeq. epist. 3, ubi et disputat, parum recte inter nos sublatam videri servitutem. Speciosum charitatis esse praetextum, sed inutilem. Hominum inde liberorum colluviem redundasse, quos licentia ac egestas ad flagitia aut mendicitatem impellat. Coarctata familiarum ministeria, carioribus aut provocacibus ingenuorum operis. Adde caedes, servitute sublata, frequentiores esse; quod Romanis in civilibus bellis experti sunt, quibus capti non sunt servi. Tacit. 2 hist. c.44, Plutarch in Othon. et 1. 21 § 1 d. capt. et postlim. Non deest his rationibus suum pondus. Videatur Berneggerus ad Taciti German. quaest. 134."

11. *Eunomia Romana,* on *D.*1.5.5.1 (Marcian, Institutes book 1); p. 49 in the Amsterdam, 1722, edition.

12. See, for example, H. Grotius, *De Jure Belli ac Pacis,* 1.1.10, 11, 12; 3.11.1; Sir George Mackenzie, *Institutions of the Law of Scotland,* 1,1; Johannes Voet, *Elementa Juris secundum ordinem Institutionum Justiniani,* 1.2. Cf. Alan Watson, "Some Notes on Mackenzie's *Institutions* and the European Legal Tradition," *Jus Commune* (1989): 1ff.

13. On the Roman use of *ius naturale* see further in Chapter 8.

14. 1.1.12.

15. "Quum praeterea jus naturae eas complectatur leges, quae universo generi per rectam rationem sunt promulgatae, homines autem, vel singuli seorsum, vel, prout in certas societates coaluerunt, considerari possint: jus, quo singulorum actiones reguntur, NATURALE; quod, quid in societatibus, et inter eas justum injustumve sit, praecipit, JUS GENTIUM vocamus; adeoque eadem juris utrius sunt praecepta, eadem leges, quin immo

Jus Gentium est ipsum jus naturale, vitae hominis sociali negotiisque societatum atque integrarum gentium adplicatum" (1.1.21. Cf. 2.1.1).

16. 1.10.275.

17. 2.4.76ff.

18. 2.4.84.

19. 2.4.88. An English divine who believed that slavery was in accordance with natural law was Thomas Rutherforth, *Institutes of Natural Law* (Cambridge, 1754), 1:474ff. This treatise may have been used by Judge Thomas Ruffin of North Carolina in the famous case of *State v. Mann*, 13 N.C. (2 Dev.) 1829, 263. Ruffin stated that "arguments drawn from the well-established principles which confer and restrain the authority of the parent over the child, the tutor over the pupil, the master over the apprentice" had been pressed upon him to determine that battery of one's own slave could be a crime. But he declared (p. 265) there was no likeness. In one case "the end in view is the happiness of the youth," in the other it is "the profit of the master, his security and the public safety." Rutherforth had claimed (p. 475) that "the good of the child is the end, to which the authority of the parent over the child is directed: and the good of the master is the end, to which the authority of the master over the slave is directed." Ruffin's own copy of Rutherforth (now in the University of North Carolina Law Library) bears his signature and the date "Nov. 22nd 1821" so it was in his possession some years before *State v. Mann*. Chapter 20, "On Slavery," is the only chapter flagged in the index. Ruffin, as a judge sensitive to the moral issues of slavery but alert to the actual conditions of life, would find Rutherforth's views on slavery of great interest and of particular practicality.

20. See Alan Watson, *The Making of the Civil Law* (Cambridge, Mass., 1981), pp. 97f.

21. See Perdigão Malheiro, *A Escravidão no Brasil*, vol. 1, 3d ed. (Petrópolis, 1976). The first edition dates from 1866–67.

22. Very few slaves in the country married, though in the cities marriages among slaves were as common as among free persons. The first official Brazilian census of 1872 showed that 10 percent of slaves were married; see S. M. De Q. Mattoso, *To Be a Slave in Brazil* (New Brunswick, 1980), p. 110, Malheiro, *Escravidão*, 1:60.

23. *Decretum. de conjugio servorum* 4.1.

24. See Malheiro, *Escravidão*, 1:60f.

25. *D.22.5.7*; Malheiro, *Escravidão*, 1:67.

26. Malheiro, *Escravidão*, 1:67.

27. See ibid., pp. 92f.

28. But evidence, of course, would be needed.

29. Argued from *Ordenaçoes Filipinas*, 5.99, and *Providência* of 29 April 1719.

30. Mattoso, *To Be a Slave*, pp. 147, 160ff.; see also M. C. Karasch, *Slave Life in Rio de Janeiro, 1808–1850* (Princeton, 1987), pp. 335ff.

31. Mattoso, *To Be a Slave*, pp. 164f. See also S. B. Schwartz, "Manumission of Slaves in Colonial Brazil," *Hispanic American Historical Review* 54 (1974): 611.

32. The decline thereafter occurred where the number of Creole slaves did not increase; see Mattoso, *To Be a Slave*, p. 164.

33. See Schwartz, "Manumission," p. 612.

34. See Mattoso, *To Be a Slave*, p. 157.

35. See Malheiro, *Escravidão*, 1:100.

36. *Ordenaçoes Filipinas* 5.36.1 Repert. das Ord. v *castigar pode.*

37. *Repert.* cit., Prov. em Res. de Conulta of 20 March 1688.

38. *Circ.* no. 263 of 1852; *Código do processo penal*, article 125.

39. Mattoso, *To Be a Slave*, p. 136.

40. *Ordenaçoes Filipinas* 5.62.1.

41. Ibid., 5.41.

42. *Providência* of 3 April 1720; *Alvara* of 3 March 1741.

43. Article 174, section 19.

44. Article 179, section 19; *Aviso* 283 of 26 June 1865.

45. *Ordenaçoes Filipinas* 4.13. In 1865 the court declared reenslavement unacceptable, but it remained legal.

46. See Mattoso, *To Be a Slave*, p. 179.

47. See above all the works of Gilberto Freyre, such as *The Masters and the Slaves* (New York, 1946), pp. 4, 18f.; *O Mundo que o portugués criou* (Rio de Janeiro, 1940).

48. See Marvin Harris, "The Myth of the Friendly Master," in Laura Foner and Eugene D. Genovese, eds., *Slavery in the New World* (Englewood Cliffs, N.J., 1969), pp. 39ff.; David B. Davis, *The Problem of Slavery in Western Culture* (Ithaca, 1966), pp. 235ff.

49. That throughout the centuries of slavery in America, Brazil was the biggest importer of slaves with 38 percent —the United States being second with only 6 percent—would suggest that the attrition rate was high. For a modern comparison of slavery in Brazil and the United States see Carl N. Degler, *Neither Black nor White* (New York, 1971).

7. SLAVE LAW IN DUTCH AMERICA

1. Similarly obscure is the history of slave law in the Dutch East India Company's colony in southern Africa at the Cape; see G. G. Visagie, *Regspleging en Reg aan die Kaap* (Cape Town, 1969), pp. 88ff. The general conclusion (from van Wessels, *History of the Roman-Dutch Law* [Grahamstown, 1908], p. 412) is that Roman law prevailed with great modifications in the Dutch possessions. But Visagie expressly says that at the Cape itself the position was not so clear (*Regspleging*, p. 89 n. 96). For A. M. Hugo, the practice was very similar to that at Rome (*The Cape Vernacular* [Inaugural lecture, University of Cape Town, 1970]). The position at the Cape, where the Statute van Batavia (1642) applied, is not the same as that of Dutch America. See also Nigel Worden, *Slavery in Dutch South Africa* (Cambridge 1985), pp. 101 ff., 115, 143ff.; Robert Ross, *Cape of Torments: Slavery and Resistance in South Africa* (London, 1983).

2. The charter is in Cornelius Cau's edition of the *Groot Placaet-Boek*, 1 (1658), pp. 565ff.

3. Article 56: "De Civile Justitie over allerley actien reële ende personele, sal werden gheadministreert by drie Commissarissen vande Raede, daer toe by het Collegie to committeren van drie tot drie Maenden, ende dat by ommeganghe, die daer in sullen volgen van ghelijcken de ghemeene ordre vande Vereenighte Provintien, ofte soodanige als by de Vergaderinge vande Negenthiene sal goet gevonden worden; doch de proceduren soo kort ende sommier maecken, sonder lange treyneringe, als eenighsints nae de natur van saecken, ende parthyen on verkort, doenlijck sal wesen" (*Groot Plakaet-Boek*, 2 (1664), pp. 1235ff. at p. 1244.

4. See H. R. Hahlo and E. Kahn, *The South African Legal System and Its Background* (Cape Town, 1973), p. 515.

5. These will be found listed in the index under the heading *Slaven* in the *General Register over de Negen Deelen van het Groot Placaatboek* (1797), p. 596.

6. See Simon van Leeuwen, *Paratitula juris novissimi, dat is, Een kort begrip van het Rooms-Hollants Reght* (1652); Van Leeuwen, *Het Roomsch Hollandsh Recht* (1664).

7. See Hugo Grotius, *Inleiding tot de Hollandsche Rechtsgeleertheyd* (1631).

8. See Ulrich Huber, *Heedendaegse Rechtsgeleertheyt* (1686).

9. "In andere saecken van allerley Contracten ende handelingen, sullen gevolght werden de gemeene beschreven Rechten."

10. "Servitutem Curassoviae obtinere, et hanc esse coloniam sub auspiciis et imperio Ordinum Generalium, ibi, paucis exceptis, vigere jus Romanum ex § 61 formae regiminis, quam Ordines Generales Societati Occidentali praescripserunt 13 October 1629 (Plac. 2, p. 1235) vigere igitur leges de servis, et quicquid de servis fugitivis constituitur toto tit. ff. et C. de servis fugit." (*Observationes Tumultuariae*, no. 2966, (in 4:41f.). This work was first published, edited by E. M. Meijers, A. S. de Blécourt, and H. D. J. Bodenstein in 1926 to 1962.

11. "Attamen hoc ius minime est extendendum est ad servos, qui a dominis suis e Coloniis aufugerunt, auippe qui hoc illicito facto, etiamsi in Belgium advenerint, libertatem non adipiscuntur, verum dominis restituendi est." ("But this right is not at all to be extended to slaves who fled from their owners from the colonies, because after this illicit act they do not acquire liberty, even if they arrive in Belgium, but they are to be returned to their owners") in *Johannes Voet, Commentarii ad Pandectas, tomus 3: continens Supplementum auctore Joanne van der Linden, Sectio Prima, a libro 1 usque ad 12 Pandectarum* (1793), 1.5.3.

12. Among the works I have consulted are J. de Sande (1568–1638), *Decisionum Frisicarum Libri Duo*; I. van den Berg (active in practice in Amsterdam at least between 1664 and 1691), *Neder-Lands Advys-Boek inhoudende verscheide Consultatien en Advysen van voorname Rechtsgeleerden in Neder-Land*, 4 vols. (1693–96); L. van Lanckeren, *Utrechtse Consultatien*, 4 vols. (1st ed., 1671); J. Schrassert (1687–1756), *Consultatien, Advysen ende Advertissementen*, 5 vols., J. Schrassert, *Practicae Observationes*, 2 vols.; *Consultatien, Advysens en Advertissementen gegeven en geschreven by Verscheide Treffelyke Rechtsgeleerden in Holland*, 6 vols. (1716); G. de Haas, *Nieuwe Hollandsche Consultatien* (1741); E. van Zurck, *Codex Batavus* (1st ed., 1711), s.v. *Slaven*.

13. It is hard to see what issues in slave law other than the status of runaways could come before the courts of the United Provinces.

14. For Surinam, see *West Indisch Placaatboek: Plakaten, Ordonnantiën en andere Wetten, uitgevaardigd in Suriname*, pt. 1, ed. by J. Th. de Smidt (Amsterdam, 1973), e.g., nos. 8 (1669, pp. 27f.); 149 (1689, pp. 184ff.); 211 (1701, p. 244); for Curaçao, see *West Indisch Placaatboek: Publikaties en andere Wetten alsmede de oudste Resoluties betrekking hebbende op Curaçao, Aruba, Bonaire*, 1, ed. by J. Th. de Smidt, T. van der Lee and J. A. Schiltkamp (Amsterdam, 1978), e.g. nos. 66 (1710, pp. 101f.); 76 (1713, p. 115); 173 (1743, pp. 231f.); for St. Maarten, see *West Indisch Plakaatboek: Publikaties en andere Wetten betrekking hebbende op St.*

Maarten, St. Eustatius, Saba, edit. by J. Th. de Smidt and T. van der Lee (Amsterdam, 1979), e.g., nos. 82 (1777, pp. 78ff.); 93 (1779, pp. 89f.).

15. For Surinam, see, e.g., 1, nos. 244 (1711, p. 280); 297 (1722, pp. 348f.); 348 (1733, p. 409); 553 (1741, pp. 663ff.); 2, (Amsterdam, 1973), no. 591 (1761, pp. 721f.).

16. For Surinam, see 1, e.g., nos. 263 (1714, pp. 302f.); 378 (1738, pp. 445ff.); 477 (1748, pp. 578f.); 2, e.g., nos. 601 (1761, pp. 731f.); 785 (1788, p. 942); for St. Maarten, no. 85 (1778, pp. 82f.) for St. Eustatius, no. 80 (1790, pp. 340f.).

17. For Surinam, see 1, e.g., no. 312 (1724, pp. 368ff.); 2, e.g., nos. 659 (1764, p. 785); 697 (1768, p. 816); 698 (1769, p. 817); 728 (1773, p. 851); 881 (1785, pp. 1078f.).

18. For Curaçao, see 1, e.g., nos. 170 (1743, pp. 229f.); 266 (1761, pp. 319f.); 308 (1770, pp. 372ff.; 2 (Amsterdam, 1978), nos. 382 (1789, pp. 454ff.); 391 (1791, pp. 462ff.).

19. For Surinam, see 1, e.g., nos. 292 (1721, pp. 342f.); 499 (1753, pp. 605ff.); 2, no. 630 (1762, p. 755).

20. For Surinam, see 1, e.g., no. 336 (1730, p. 398).

21. For Surinam, see 1, e.g., no. 400 (1741, p. 481), 2, e.g., no. 589 (1761, pp. 716ff.).

22. For Surinam, see 1, e.g., no. 574 (1760, pp. 690f.); 2, nos. 591 (1761, pp. 721f.); 700 (1769, p. 819); 838 (1781, pp. 1006f.).

23. For Surinam, see 1, e.g., no. 580 (1760, pp. 696f.); 2, e.g., nos. 696 (1767, p. 815); 701 (1769, p. 820); 746 (1774, p. 871); 748 (1774, p. 876); 808 (1779, p. 967: being on a particular road with a gun).

24. For Surinam, see 1, e.g., no. 442 (1745, pp. 538f.); 2, e.g., nos. 610 (1761, p. 741); 705 (1770, p. 825); 706 (1770, pp. 825f.); 824 (1780, p. 988).

25. For Surinam, see, e.g., 2, nos. 609 (1761, pp. 739f.); 639 (1763, p. 769: for shooting a runaway dead); 750 (1775, p. 877).

26. For Surinam, see 1, e.g., no. 492 (1750, pp. 595ff.); [cf. no. 534 (1757, p. 644)]; 2, e.g., nos. 660 (1764, p. 786); 679 (1766, p. 800); 704 (1700, p. 824); 727 (1773, p. 850); 736 (1773, p. 862); 753 (1775, p. 879); 756 (1775, p. 881); 769 (1776, pp. 899f.); 770 (1776, pp. 900ff.); 855 (1781, pp. 1035f.); 880 (1784, p. 1077); 885 (1786, pp. 1106f.); 890 (1787, p. 1116); 904 (1791, pp. 1148ff.).

27. For Surinam, see 2, e.g., no. 713 (1771, pp. 832f.).

28. For Surinam, see 2, e.g., nos. 729 (1773, p. 852); 761 (1775, p. 889); 823 (1780, pp. 987f.); for Curaçao, see 2, e.g., no. 442 (1795, pp. 514ff.).

29. For Surinam, see 2, e.g., nos. 838 (1781, pp. 1006f.); 924 (1794, p. 1181); for St. Maarten, no. 60 (1770 pp. 61ff.).

30. For Surinam, see 2, e.g., no. 811 (1780, pp. 971f.).

31. For Curaçao, see 1, e.g., nos. 133 (1738, p. 184); 250 (1756, pp. 301ff.); for St. Eustatius, see, e.g., no. 81 (1790, pp. 341f.).

32. For Curaçao, see 1, e.g., nos. 297 (1769, pp. 355ff.; 300 (1769, pp. 360f.).

33. 1, no. 65 (1710, pp. 100f.).

34. 1, no. 159 (1742, pp. 222f.).

35. 1, no. 296 (1769, pp. 353ff.).

36. This difficulty of distinguishing free men from slaves is expressly given as the reason for a very different rule at Rome (*D*.18.1.4, 5).

37. No. 67 (1773, pp. 68f.).

38. No. 70 (1775, pp. 71f.); cf. no. 87 (1779, p. 84) concerning sugar.

39. No. 78 (1790, pp. 339f.).

40. No. 109 (1798, pp. 375f.).

41. 1, no. 528 (1757, pp. 638f.).

42. See, e.g., 1, no. 558 (1759, pp. 676f.); 2, no. 593 (1761, pp. 722f.). With regard to bad practices in the trading in slaves see, e.g., 1, no. 507 (1754, p. 615).

43. See, e.g., 2, no. 684 (1766, pp. 804f.), which applies also to other important effects.

44. See 2, no. 689 (1767, pp. 808f.).

45. There were other *placaaten* to different effects restricting owners. Thus those who had slaves suffering from particular named diseases had to keep them at home; e.g., 1, no. 583 (1761, pp. 707f.).

46. See, e.g., H. D. Benjamins and J. F. Snelleman, *Encyclopaedie van Nederlandsch West-Indië* (The Hague, Leiden, 1914–17), s.v. Slavernij, pp. 637ff., esp. p. 641.

47. I cannot refrain from an analogy. The Berkeley campus of the University of California is the only one I know where there are signs forbidding the bringing of dogs into classrooms. This does not mean the authorities there are more hostile to dogs than are the trustees of other universities. Rather, it reflects a more relaxed attitude toward dogs. At Berkeley, but not elsewhere, it might be thought that dogs were acceptable in class.

48. 1, no. 67 (1710, pp. 102f.).

49. 1, no. 116 (1737, pp. 164f.).

50. 1, no. 150 (1741, p. 218).

51. See, e.g., 1, no. 288 (1766, pp. 337f.). A few days later, whites were forbidden to fight: 1, no. 289 (1766, pp. 338f.).

52. See 1, no. 290 (1767, pp. 340f.).

53. See, e.g., 1, no. 330 (1779, pp. 395f.).

54. See 1, no. 133 (1738, p. 184).

55. See, e.g., 1, nos. 209 (1749, pp. 265f.); 259 (1757, pp. 311f.). Whites were ordered to respect blacks and mulattoes who were serving in the watch.

56. See, e.g., 2, no. 768 (1776, pp. 898f.).

57. 1, no. 240 (1711, p. 277).

58. 2, no. 862 (1782, p. 1048).

59. See, e.g., 2, no. 772 (1777, pp. 904f.). For mustering to control free blacks see, e.g., 2, no. 719 (1772, p. 840).

60. See e.g., 1, nos. 143 (1740, pp. 208f.); 216 (1750, pp. 270ff.).

61. "Wij Izaac Faesch Gouverneur over Curaçao ende derselver on-derhoorige districten mitsgaders den Edele Achtbaare Raade deeses ey-lands.

"Allen dengeenen die deesen zullen zien ofte hooren leesen (salut); doen te weeten alzoo de moetwilligheyt der slaaven, zoo neegers als moulatten, hier te landen (nietteegenstaande de voorsieninge door ons daarteegens ge-daan bij 't placcaat gearresteert den 17 october 1740) daagelijks grooter werden, zoodanigh dat gemelde neegers en moulatten zig in troupen en parthijen verdeelen en op het praesuppoost van versogt te sijn op be-gravenisse, bruyloften en andere zoogenaamde combites, mitsgaders zig niet meer en schaamen omme bij daage en nagte de goede ingeseetenen alhier te ontrusten, qualijk te bejeegenen ende met veragting te behandelen, booven en behalven het onbehoorlijk leeven van de voorszegde neegers en moulatten zoo in Willemstad, buyten de Steenepadspoort, aan de oversijde van deese haaven, als op de werven en plantagien, omme te saamen te rot-ten, te speelen op trommels en instrumenten en zig met dansen en dron-kendrinken beezig houden. Welke bijeenkomste van schadelijke gevolgen sijn en occagien geeven tot vegterije met messen, stocken, vuysten en di-ergelijke, mitsgaders van nog andere en meerdere pernicieuse consequen-tien en nademaal diergelijke tumultueuse aanslagen ende seditieuse actien van zwaare gevolgen koomen te zijn en het dierhalven van veel noodsaake-lijkheyt is omme daarinne ten spoedigste te voorsien.

"(Zoo is't) dat Gouverneur en Raaden bij deesen statueeren en ordon-neeren.

"1. Dat geene slaaven zoo neegers als moulatten bij elkander en van nu voortaan zoo in Willemstad, buyten de Steenpadspoort, aan de oversijde van deese haaven als elders, zoo bij daagen als nagten zullen vergaderen op eenige conventiculen ofte zoogenaamde combites, veel minder op trommels, vioolen off andere instrumenten te speelen, te dansen ofte eenige vlaggen uyt te steeken, op paene van dadelijk geapprehendeert en strengelijk met waterpana te werden geslaagen ofte andersints swaarder straffe naar bevindinge van zaaken.

"2. Dat geene begraaffenisse van slaaven van meer neegers off moulatten zullen moogen werden geadsisteert als van ses persoonen, die na de begravinge aanstonds na haar huys sullen moeten vertrecken, op paene als vooren.

"3. Geene neegers off moulatten hiervooren genoemt sullen vermoogen na 9 uuren des nagts op straat te passeeren als voorsien sijnde met een biljet van haar meester off meesteres geteekent, op paene als booven, opdat geen dieverije werden gepleegd.

"4. Dat op deese gantschen eyland zoo door blanken als vrije neegers en moulatten, veel minder door eenige slaaven, voor de slaaven, zoo neegers als moulatten, niet zullen moogen werden getapt, vrolikheyt op te regten en vlaggen uyt te steeken, op paene voor de blanken voor de eerste rijs van een boete van pezos 50, voor de tweede rijs op dubbelde boete en dat haare neering sal werden verbooden voor een jaar ende voor de darde rijse op paene van pezos 300 en dat de neering voor altoos aan den overtreeder van 't selve verbooden zal worden. Ten opsigte van de vrije neegers en moulatten dat haar dit eyland zal werden ontzegt ende met de eerste occaie versonden, ende laastelijk voor de slaaven, zoo neegers als moulatten, strengelijk met waterpana te werden geslaagen.

"5. Geen van de voorszegde slaaven zullen vermoogen teegens den andere te vegten met vuysten, stocken, messen off andere geweer, in geenderlije maniere, op paene van gestraft te werden zoo Haar Edele Achtbaare zullen vermeenen te behooren.

"6. Dog zoo deselve vegterije koor de voorszegde slaaven teegens blanken ondernoomen worden oftewel eenige scherp treckende teegens blanken, als van ouds op dit eyland gebruikelijk is geweest.

"7. Geene blanken off vrije neegers en moulatten zullen van nu voortaan geen schiet- en zijdgeweer van wat benaaming die ook mogte sijn, mitsgaders cruyt en lood off eenige andere krijgsamunitie aan slaaven, zoo neegers als moulatten, hebben te geeven ofte te verkoopen als op geteekende briefjes van haar meesters, op paene voor de blanken van de vrije negers en moulatten van dit eyland te werden gebannen ofte wel zwaarder straffe zoo bevonden zal werden te behooren.

"Lastende ende bevellende den provisioneele fiscaal deeser eylanden en

desselfs substituit schout provisioneel omme deesen na de letter te ex-
ecuteeren ende ordoneerende Haar Edele Achtbaare wel scherpelijk de cap-
itainen van de vrije negers en moulatten omme de justitie kennisse te geeven
van de plaats en persoonen die contrarie deeses mogte koomen te ageeren,
alzoo wij hetzelve voor dit eyland en alle desselfs goede ingeseetenen tot
voorkominge van verdere onheylen ende tot eene gematigde decipline onder
de slaaven hebben geoordeelt alzoo te behooren.

Aldus———"

62. See, e.g., 1, nos. 215 (1750, p. 270); 292 (1767, pp. 342f.).

63. See no. 86 (1779, pp. 83f.).

64. 1, no. 442 (1795, pp. 514ff.).

65. A short account of each known Roman statute will be found in
Giovanni Rotondi, *Leges publicae populi romani* (1922; rpt. Hildesheim,
1966).

66. We might compare modern textbooks of English law on contract or
property, which also do not discuss administrative regulations.

67. E. Bentura Belaña, *Autos Acordados* (1787), no. 82, pp. 72f.

68. Ibid., no. 83, p. 73.

69. Ibid., no. 84, p. 73.

70. Ibid., no. 87, p. 74.

71. 1, no. 350 (pp. 411f.). "Allen dengeenen die deesen sullen sien ofte
hooren leesen saluyt; doen te weeten als dat bij ons in overweeging ge-
nomen zijnde het veelvuldige vrijgeve van slaven en mulatten en 't ac-
cresseeren van dien, de menigvuldige quade gevolgen die er veelteyds uyt
werden georieerd, aengesien deselve gemanumitteerde sijnde sig veeltijds
niet ontsien om sig evenswel met dienstbare te vermengen door dron-
kenschap, quade conduites, deselve debaucheeren tot groot nadeel der
eygenaeren.

"Soo is 't dat wij deese saak wel rijpelick overwoogen hebbende, hebben
goedgevonden om dit volgende reglement ten opsigte der vrij te gevene persoonen te publiceeren, waarnaar een eyder in 't toekoomende sig sal hebben
te reguleeren.

"1. Niemand sal vermoogen, hetsij wie het ook weesen mogte, eenige
mulatten ofte neegers te manumitteeren, 't sij bij testamente off andersints,
sonder voorgaende permissie en goedkeuringe van den Edele Hove van Politie etc., dewelke ook niet aengenoomen sullen werden bevorens deselve in
staat sijn haer cost te kunnen winnen, ten eynde sij bij faute vandien niet
komen te vervallen ten lasten van de colonie.

"2. Die uyt hunne slavernije gemanumitteerd worden blijven egter gehouden gelijk meede haare kinderen en descendenten, hunnen patronen en vrouwen, mitsgaders serselver kinderen en descendenten alle ere, respect ende reverentien te bewijsen.

"3. Ende in cas de gemanumitteerde zijn patroon ofte vrouwe komen te slaen, injurieren ofte eenige smaet aen deselve mogte doen, daarvan valeable blijken sijnde, soo sal denselven weder in dienstbaarheyd en slavernij ten voordeel van haare geweesene patroon off patroonesse vervalle.

"4. Dat alle dengeene, wie het ook weesen mogten, versoekende aen den Edele Hove de vrijheyd van een eenig slaaff, sig sullen moeten obligeeren om deselve in de christelijke religie te doen onderwijsen en opbrengen.

"5. Soo sijn ook de gemanumitteerde gehouden hunne patronen mitsgaders derselver kinderen en verdere descendenten, in armoede vervallen sijnde, naar hun vermogen ende geleegentheyd alimenteeren, namentlijk onderhoud te versorgen ter taexatie van den regter.

"6. Ook sullen de gemanumitteerde onder sigh off wel andersints mogen trouwen, except uytgesondert met persoonen die in slavernij zijn.

"7. De gemanumitteerde deese wereld overlijdende, sullen haar wettige lijffsgeboorte en verdere descendenten in inffinitum, soo eenige hebben, in alle derselver nagelatene goederen succedeeren op den voet van 't aasdomsregt.

"8. Dat alle vrijgegeven mulatten, indianen, neegers en negerinnen die sig met slaaven off slaavinnen mogte koomen te vermengen en daermeede kinderen te procreeren, dat voor de eerste reyse sullen werden gemuliteert met een arbitraire pecunieele boete, de helffte voor den heer raed fiscael en d'andere helffte voor 't hosptiall, de tweede reyse met corporeele correctie en de derde reyse in voorige slaavernij gereedegeerdt.

"9. Maar en gemanumitteerde van sijn nagelaate goderen bij uytterste wille willende beveelen sal sulx mogen doen, mits dat soo wanneer geen kinderen als voorszegt nalaten gehouden sullen sijn hunne patronen off derselver kinderen te institueeren in een geregte vierde part van derselver nalatenschap.

"Ende opdat niemand hiervan eenige ignorantie soude hebben ofte kunnen preetendeeren, sal deese almomme werde gepubliceerdt ende geaffigeert ter plaetse, daer men gewoon is soodaenige publicatie en affixtie te doen."

72. See, e.g., Alan Watson, *Roman Slave Law* (Baltimore, 1987), pp. 37ff.

73. See, e.g., J.1.16.1; D.25.3.6.1; 40.9.30.

74. C.6.3.1.

75. *J*.3.7.

76. 1, no. 394 (1741, pp. 471f.).

77. 2, no. 597 (1761, pp. 726f.).

8. SOME COMPARISONS

1. See David B. Davis, *The Problem of Slavery in Western Culture* (Ithaca, 1966), p. 234.

2. By me too: see Alan Watson, book review, *Yale Law Journal* 91 (1982): 1044.

3. See Alan Watson, *The Making of the Civil Law* (Cambridge, Mass., 1981), pp. 10ff.; Watson, *Failures of the Legal Imagination* (Philadelphia, 1988), pp. 47f.

4. See Cicero, *De legibus*, 1.17–37, 2.8–15; *De re publica*, 3.21, 32–34; *De harispicum responso*, 32.

5. "3. Ius naturale est, quod natura omnia animalia docuit: nam ius istud non humani generis proprium, sed omnium animalium, quae in terra, quae in mari nascuntur, avium quoque commune est. hinc descendit maris atque feminae coniunctio, quam nos matrimonium appellamus, hinc liberorum procreatio, hinc educatio: videmus etenim cetera quoque animalia, feras etiam istius juris peritia censeri. 4. Ius gentium est, quo gentes humanae utuntur. quod a naturali recedere facile intellegere licet, quia illud omnibus animalibus, hoc solis hominibus inter se commune sit."

6. "Libertas est naturalis facultas eius quod cuique facere libet, nisi si quid vi aut iure prohibetur. Servitus est constitutio iuris gentium, qua quis dominio alieno contra naturam subicitur. 2. Servi ex eo appellati sunt, quod imperatores captivos vendere ac per hoc servare nec occidere solent."

7. See Watson, *Making of the Civil Law*, pp. 84ff. Justinian's *Institutes*, 2.1.37, states that by natural law the offspring of animals belongs to the usufructuary. This would suggest that the keeping of animals is regarded as being in accordance with natural law, but it should be noted that the text of the jurist Gaius (in *D*.22.1.18.2), from which the passage derives, contains no mention of natural law.

8. At *J*.1.2.*pr*.; 1.3.1, 2.

9. "Sed naturalia quidem iura, quae apud omnes gentes peraeque servantur, divina quadam providentia constituta, semper firma atque immutabilia permanent: ea vero quae ipsa sibi quaeque civitas constituit, saepe mutari solent vel tacito consensu populi vel alia postea lege lata."

10. See above all, Contardo Ferrini, *Opere* (Milan, 1929), 2:334.

11. This approach to *ius naturale* (and its closeness to *ius gentium*) is confirmed if we can accept the *Paraphrase* of Theofilus as giving Justinianic attitudes: 1.2 *pr.*, 11; 1.3.1, 2.

12. "Aman e cobdician, naturalmente, todas las criaturas del mundo, la libertad, quanto mas los omes que han entendimiento sobre todas las otras, e mayormente en aquellos que son de noble coraçon."

13. "Servidumbre, es postura, e establescimiento, que fizieron antiquamente las gentes, por la qual los omes que eran naturalmente libres se fazen siervos: e se meter a señorio de otro, contra razon de natura. E siervo tomo este nome de una palabra que llamen en latin, servare: que quier tanto dezir en romance, como guardar. E esta guarda fue establescida por los emperadores. Ca antiguamente todos quantos cativavan: matavan."

14. Alan Watson, *Roman Slave Law* (Baltimore, 1987), p. 8.

15. "Servidumbre es la mas vil, e la mas despreciada cosa, que entre los omes puede ser. Porque el ome, que es la mas noble, e libre criatura, entre todas las otras criaturas, que dios fizo, se torna por ella en poder de otro: de guisa que pueden fazer delo que quieseren, como de otro su aver bivo, o muerto." For a typical misunderstanding of the point of the Spanish texts that slavery is contrary to natural law, see A. Levaggi, "La condición juridica del esclavo en la epoca hispanica," *Revista de Historia del Derecho* 1 (1973): 83ff. at p. 149.

16. "Ius naturale en latin, tanto quiere dezir en romance, como derecho natural, que han en si los omes naturalmente, e aun las otras animalias, que han sentido. Ca segund el movimiento deste derecho, el masculo se ayunta con la fembra, e que nos llamamos casamiento, e por el crian los omes a sus fijos, e todas las animalias. Otrosi ius gentium en latin: tanto quiere dezir, como derecho comunal de todas las gentes el qual conviene a los omes, e no a las otras animalias. E este fue hallado con razon, e otrosi por fuerça, porque los omes non podrian bien bivir entresi en concordia, e en paz si todos non usassen del."

17. Herbert Klein, *Slavery in the Americas* (Chicago, 1967), p. 38, following J. C. Hurd, *Law of Freedom and Bondage* (1858; rpt. New York, 1968), pp. 40ff.

18. It was at times argued that black Africans were not human: see Louis Sala-Molins, *Le code noir ou le calvaire de Canaan* (Paris, 1987), pp. 25ff.

19. It is not my intention to discuss in detail here the various bases proposed for regarding Spanish American law as not concerning chattel slavery, but it must be observed that Klein's account of the legal rules is inaccurate in several regards (*Slavery*, p. 61).

20. Indeed, the difficulty that seems to be experienced in finding a sufficiently descriptive name for this supposed other kind of slavery is revealing.

21. Lofft 1, 98 Eng. Rep. 499 (KB. 1772).

22. See William M. Wiecek, "*Somerset*: Lord Mansfield and the Legitimacy of Slavery in the Anglo-American World," *University of Chicago Law Review* 42 (1974): 86ff. at pp. 88ff.; and, above all, James Oldham, "New Light on Mansfield and Slavery," *Journal of British Studies* 27 (1988): 45ff.

23. See, e.g., Wiecek, "Somerset"; Oldham, "Mansfield." For the impact of the case in America see Paul Finkelman, *An Imperfect Union* (Chapel Hill, 1981).

24. *Commentaries on the Laws of England*, 1st ed. (1765), 1:123.

25. This book has been reprinted in Paul Finkelman, ed., *Slavery, Race, and the American Legal System*, vol. 1 (New York, 1988).

26. David B. Davis does observe that in France there existed "seeming precedents" for the Somersett decision: *The Problem of Slavery in the Age of Revolution, 1770–1823* (Ithaca, 1975), pp. 505f. But he makes little of the point and does not discuss the instances dealt with by Hargrave. These "seeming precedents" are conveniently set out in T. B. Howell, *Complete Collection of State Trials* (London, 1814), 20:12ff. It is likely that they are responsible for much of the rhetoric evidenced in Somersett's case. There may be a good English precedent (which is referred to by Hargrave), though our information is too scanty to be precise, in John Rushworth, *Historical Collections* (1680), 2:468. Discussing punishments, Rushworth says: "Whipping was painful and shameful, *Flagellation* for Slaves. In the Eleventh of *Elizabeth*, one *Cartwright* brought a Slave from *Russia*, and would scourge him, for which he was questioned; and it was resolved that *England* was too pure an Air for Slaves to breath in."

27. In the first edition at p. 71.

28. *Tractatus de legibus abrogatis et inusitatis in Hollandia vicinisque regionibus* (1669), on *J*.1.8.3.

29. Especially A. Mornacius, *In Senatu Paris Patroni Observationes in XXIV Priores Libros Digestorum*, ad D.4.6.20; A. Perezius, *Praelectiones in libros XII Codicis Iustiniani*, ad C.7.25.1; Gudelinus, *De Iure novissimo* 1.4.9 (who does not believe the slaves become free, though their de facto liberty is protected); P. Christinaeus (1553–1631), *Practicarum Quaestionum Rerumque in Supremis Belgarum Curis Decisiones*, vol. 4, dec. 80.

30. *Commentarius ad Pandectas* 1.5.3.

31. Arnaldus Vinnius, *In quattuor libros Institutionum Imperialium Commentarius*, 1.3.

32. P. 72.

33. P. 42.

34. *Pandectes du Droit François* 2.2 (p. 6 in the edition of 1607).

35. In France subsequent royal edicts of October 1716 (*Code noir*, pp. 192ff.) and of December 1738 (addition to *Code noir*, pp. 481ff.) declared that (in certain circumstances) slaves brought from the colonies to France would remain slaves. Ironically, perhaps, Somersett's case was so late in England that public opinion would not allow similar remedial legislation.

36. See P. J. Mellius Freirius, *Institutiones Juris Civilis Lusitani cum publici tum privati*, 2.1.12 (vol. 2, p. 13, in the edition of Coimbra, 1859).

37. In Belgium, too, slaves coming from abroad automatically became free on reaching the country (George de Ghewiet, *Institutions du Droit belgique* [1736], 1.2.36.1). But there was an exception for the *ressort* of the Parlement of Flanders. By an edict of October 1716, published on 4 December of that year, slaves coming there from the French colonies in America remained in slavery (ibid., 1.2.36.3).

9. CONCLUSIONS ON LAW AND SOCIETY

1. See Eugen Rostowzew, s.v. *Frumentum* in *Paulys Real-Encyclopädie der classischen Altertumswissenschaft*, 7.1, 2d ed. by Georg Wissowa and Wilhelm Kroll (Stuttgart, 1910), pp. 126ff., esp. pp. 179ff.; D. Van Berchem, *Les Distributions de blé et d'argent à la plèbe romaine sous l'empire* (Geneva, 1939).

2. For the general phenomenon see Alan Watson, *Failures of the Legal Imagination* (Philadelphia, 1988), pp. 47ff.

3. But the progression toward restriction of manumission should not be regarded as continuous. In general there was an easing of manumission restrictions between 1780 and about 1810.

10. CONCLUSIONS ON SLAVERY AND SLAVE LAW

1. See Carl N. Degler, *Neither Black nor White* (New York, 1971), pp. 104ff. For the extent that this could be true in South Carolina see Larry Koger, *Black Slaveowners: Free Black Slave Masters in South Carolina, 1790–1860* (Jefferson, N.C., 1985).

INDEX

DATE DUE

MAY 3 1 2017	
	PRINTED IN U.S.A.